Tshabangu Sibusiso Malvin

Stars Do Fall in *Love*

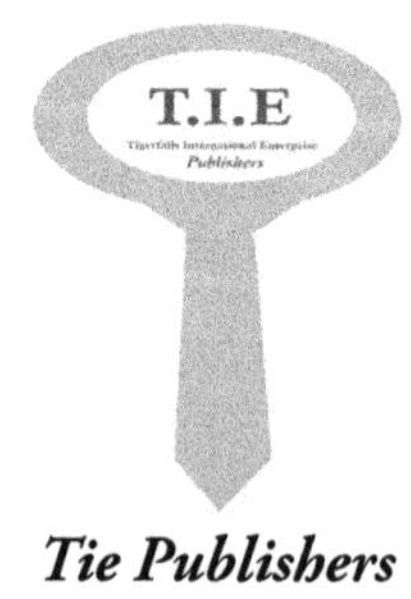

Tie Publishers

Individualism

Part One

First published by Tie Publishers 2022

First edition
ISBN: 978-0-620-94530-1
This e-book was professionally typeset by
Tie Publishers

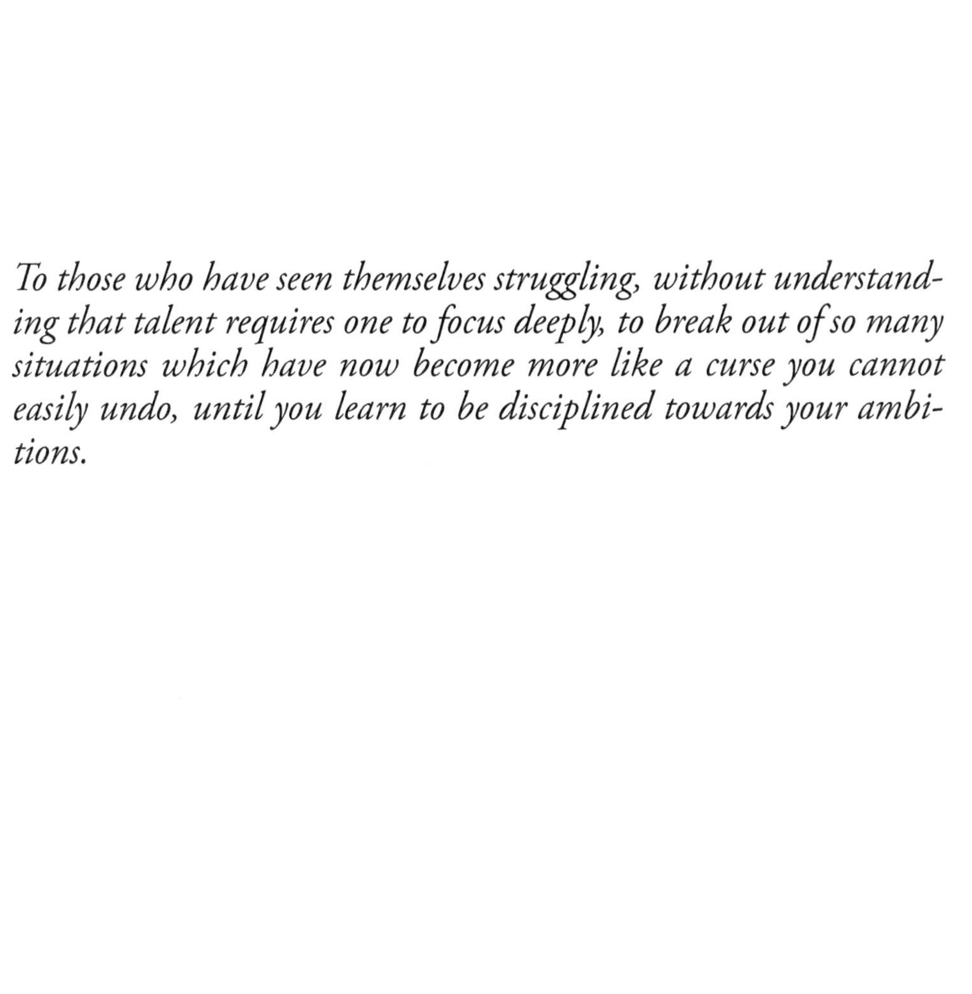

To those who have seen themselves struggling, without understanding that talent requires one to focus deeply, to break out of so many situations which have now become more like a curse you cannot easily undo, until you learn to be disciplined towards your ambitions.

Though we make too many mistakes, we're not complete failures, a lot feels like fate, however, we will not always be young, and for so much to feel as if is part of our destiny.

Table of Contents

Foreword

You can begin to work on ideas that appeals to who you are, or anything you desire most. If is something meant for the whole world, the gravity of humans can weigh down on you at some point. Along the way you may suffer the strain of having to think things thoroughly. Different mind-set might want you to understand so much clearer, which could need one to think a lot about achieving their goals precisely, and if you're not sure or persistent enough, resembling what you want. You can fail to make it out successfully.

So much can become a huge setback, through the necessity we feel to be alone when one must think of doing things accurately. You cannot make everything work normally at the same time be level with life. A lot could remain behind, and you might feel the pressure of being left back in so many activities. So in essence of creativity what people need to understand is how individualism can lead, or rather differs from isolation.

Though along the way in different stages of life, when people don't understand what they're doing, they confuse these concepts of creative intelligence. To create a world that is not certain of what they require to achieve, whereas what one needs to make sense of, is the difference that exists between us as individuals. At the beginning your desires can form as a sort of a weakness, that you have within as you try to adapt to a new life.

In some instances that period can last for a very long time, since your work won't be able to speak for you right away. It could be part of those weaknesses you've now adopted within, and the issue that many fail to understand, is when it would be able to earn you something in return. Sometimes it slips our minds to realize that time does get the better of us.

Is when you enter a stage of creativity where you refuse to ever look behind, you now have faith in what you have become. Deep within you are committed to a new way of life, is not like you can go back to the person you once were. The road leads to the deepest regions of your thoughts, on the journey to discovery, you keep on going.

Through determination that you resemble, the way never goes back, it heads to forever. You become formed by the path you travel, even when so much seems to have a hold on what you are. You keep descending deeper to knowledge that moves closer to your destiny.

So much along the way and conditions can set you up with being a failure. As the life you abandoned had been the one in which you deserved everything the world has to offer, and again, how do you prepare for the path you are to travel? Knowing that you'll go through a lot of things that could stand in your route, and without discipline. You might fall prey to different kind of situations that you wish you had been equipped for, of which you not.

Passing through that remember to remain focused ahead, and not to forget how far you traveled. It doesn't matter how you coming into the world, with life or nothing, the thing is that being the best will always find a way to succeed, and you need to arrive there.

A side of you knows that it won't come easy, for we are not birthed within that area of existence. From where we are born naturally, we are offered a certain path designed for human beings to travel, which is easy to reach success. With discipline and determination, you just focus and the next day you there.

As for the journey to self-discovery, towards perfection and being different from the rest. Is unique and individually separated from everything you have ever known, it questions a lot about what you understand or stands for. How far are you prepared to give yourself to see all that you desire happens? From here to there, just to satisfy the eager to live a very satisfactory life which you deserve, that you know you must achieve.

It takes everything for someone to get to that level. Whether physical or spiritual it needs one to enlarge their mental capacity, and you know that to find the strength to reach that horizon won't happen overnight. Immediately the mind begins to conceive success through your understanding. The universe rearranges so much for you to be different from the rest.

You don't just think about something or being unlike so many and then the next morning you have arrived, without motivation that has driven you there. What is it that you mastered which allowed your mind to step out of the ordinary, and what were the odds to defy to where you wanted to be, was it a plain path to travel or they were gatekeepers waiting to tell you how you are not of that world? As you not heading into the unknown.

You traveling to some place with human beings who are very distinctive, no one has ever been alone at the end. We could be separated by the concepts we need to represent for us to get there, not the lifestyle. There are people with similar lives to the one you desire most, and you could only be related by your ways of living, and not the activities you partake in.

So many times you will think about your goals, and how to achieve them. With so much still standing in your way, and then ask yourself, how can you have a clear path? One which cannot be distracted, and is just here for you to travel through. When the desire is within, and the way seems to be hard to reach, how can you get there?

Is every form of creativity that we master that has a good chance of helping us reach for our ambitions. To that place where we want to be, and does it matter how many paths are available, that can get us where we want to, what is it that can earn you your desired lifestyle? Your only goal, the objective you have for life that stand above everything.

Which is the concept that has separated you from the rest of the people, and knowing how to set the time frame. Will you be able to manage the duration of your projects very well in your quest to be more? You need to live as well, the vision mustn't blind you, to overlook your present situation forever.

The issue of how to reach at that place, can you arrive early, or you can spend years lost in spirit and trying to get things right? Knowing that you have it within you. However things are just not as easy as you thought they'll be, and remember that this is breaking out of the barriers of the ordinary life, into a new level of understanding.

Not just standing out from the rest, to stand apart doesn't compare with the individualism of concepts and thoughts. You equip yourself to be the best, you constantly question your integrity, how much is enough efforts to give or have?

Is not coming from behind just to fit into someone's ideas. You passing a lot of levels to be at the one which you desire, of success formed by your intelligence, and always ask this time and again;

What is an acceptable level of understanding which you require to accomplish your goals, what is enough to understand for you to reach to where you want to, do you just wake up and the next day you there, how much do you need to give to fulfill that desire? While keeping the rule of life, and knowing is not to be compromised.

You break out of the ordinary circumstances and you master your mind. You strive for what you believe in, and what is rightfully yours, and you acknowledge that without mastering a certain way of living you can never live to your best. Everything is depended on that and the efforts you need to adapt.

You want to be more than just a person struggling with understanding how to be the best. You aiming for the stars, you have the eager to showcase your talent and be something more, you believe in yourself and that you have it in you to reach that level of satisfaction. At some point it doesn't matter what you go through to get there, whatever it takes, with all the capabilities that it requires, you are willing to resemble that.

Deep within you wonder where the way leads to, as at times all we have is the eagerness to be what we love, how things will turn out from there is something hidden from us. How can you achieve perfect success with your concepts, knowing what it takes, do you have the discipline to master the complexity of situations the way you need to?

Do you have what is essential to succeed to the next stage? Against all odds, and it might happen that regardless of what you know. So much might want to stand in your way, and you are a first-timer, you are not born in that world, and you feel dropped and rejected. Can your knowledge pass with you through that to the other side, can it pick you up from everything that might want to drop you permanently?

As much as that level is not where we are born, is not our comfort zone, is our ultimate destination, created by our mind seeking its salvation. Is not our natural platform, where we are favored by everything, here we are limited. At birth we are given an area of life, more like a playground, where all our discipline routines are supposed to lead us to success.

This is our life path, formed by the vision we have, one you have chosen for yourself, and that can weigh you down so much towards that place where you need to get to. You have to be mentally prepared for the kind of exposure you'll go through, and be very determined. As it is something not common about who we are, and you are on your own in that journey. A lot of people cannot be there for you as you require them to, is yours alone, it doesn't align with what everyone is.

There is no difficulty or curse at birth, we are all given a clear path to success. The right to be born leads somewhere good and deserving of all that the world has to offer, a path not meant to suffocate us. A good and a comfortable way to live, what strains the energy out of someone is when your road is not heading towards that place common about everyone.

Is our desire to more of everything, to where life is full of abundance, is that which changes things as we have known them. So if you constantly experienced a lot of difficulties, it could be that you have always been on your journey, living through your vision, even before you became conscious of it.

It could've been something that lived with you, and it had determined the path you traveled from your early years. You have been carrying the beauty within, and the exciting part about it is that if you pass, no one ever goes back. It will be the heritage of your life and the generation after you, and if everyone finds it comfortable you keep expanding the idea, unless you have found a need to change and create a new horizon.

Otherwise is the end of all our troubles and the beginning of a new chapter, our happiness and perfect life. Created by the goal that exists inside and beyond this world, and what people see. A desire that has long lived within us, and is not controlled by anything. Is mastered out of everything through understanding, and a new world emerges, if you only strive to master the ambition, then you would've arrived.

Although you may at times find it as too impossible and hard to reach, is not. It can feel as if it has been delayed by time, only for you to understand how to truly become what you love, and figure out all the paths that exist to that place where you need to be. Is not to be confused with just trying to stand out, or being fortunate the easy way, is what you loved for the rest of your life that became what you are at the end.

Yet you feel isolated from the way you see things, and you're scared like you have been found with a crime that has built a home in you. That resides in your sub consciousness, and you are guilty of not being common in society and to other human beings, and as hard as it may be you're so keen to achieve that. The thing is nothing can ever stand in our way forever, you learn to hold on tight to your end goals.

Never let go, as difficult as it may seem, you will be given opportunities, that you must seize, and as long as it isn't where we were born to play. It might be useful to make use of that, and you require the discipline to realize that part and coming back to life with it. Always remember, and keep it in mind that chances will be there, you only need to open your eyes and be focused as you must bring all that you are. In terms of understanding how to make use of that and reach your desire.

Preface

So much you can find a way on how to be, although there are things which you may suffer from. When life calls for you to always focus on what you know how to do, you could end up suffering the consequences of being an innovative person. Alone most of your time, and sadden by the situation you find yourself in.

Whereas what's important to understand is that there could be a need to focus on what you love about the world around you. Still, it doesn't have to be at the sacrifice of your happiness. Isolation is invented by lack of understanding of what it really means to be different or to have value in creativity.

You could be more than what so many have seen, and challenged by situations you find yourself alone, and searching for who you are. While what you need is to find a way to handle such a challenge of having a different mind-set, of possessing a gift that seeks a way to life. Yes it could require one to understand things clearly, and be very productive. Therefore a need to take some time to go through things thoroughly could emerge, to see what impact or effect your idea will have in society, and the world at large.

The time you may require to understand things well, could reflect not being the same as compared to other human beings. It could indicate a different behaviour from what is expected of someone, and that's how a lot of issues might emerge, or rather be hard to deal with.

They could arise from lacking understanding with what we have become, yes from deep within, every person is unique and unlike the other. Some things could be the way we apply our routine to stand apart from the rest, and that being the reason why people treat you unfamiliar to others.

It could be something strange, but why suffering is invented from the difference that we possess, or resemble towards everything that we do. More like embracing the value of being unique is your downfall and you have to be penalized for it. While to be individually different from another mustn't be seen as a setback, to have your way of thinking subjected can isolate a human being. Just the way you don't respond to life in a similar manner, can make you feel like you're not good enough.

To be isolated from human beings and those you love, and it could insist to remain like that from the ideas we possess. As part of our creative understanding, how you look at life. Deep within to be an individual is a point of view that resembles your positive way of confronting things around you. It is mostly this kind of perspective, of innovative thinking that individualism applies to. Where someone has created value in their mental capacity and working towards being recognized, for what they understand.

We are sometimes required to show what we know, and care for in life, especially if you believe that you have a gift that is more unique and different than what others are, which mustn't be overlooked. As it is going to be a great part of human lives, and that's how we find the capabilities being valued in essence.

Is not something common about us people, except that it is found within specific individuals that possess such an excellent way of life. It could be different from so many, however there's no need to push human beings or make them feel unwelcome for what they are. As for so many can think of themselves like they don't fit in the context of ordinary, and is just a simple shift in the way you see things, or how you view the world.

We become so much, and we are no longer what people know of us, you enter a new level where you are the only one who understands what you are, and is not a bad way of making a living. So how do you accept yourself? Or adjust to situations in the manner that you are, as you won't respond to circumstances in a way that is deemed normal.

Another thing to be considered is how life is designed for common people, the difference that one possesses might be seen as if it doesn't belong, whereas you do, you're part of the idea that you value. How do you make it count as well, or push it into the context of humanity, so that it is seen exactly the way it is and what it stands for?

Since there has to be a way that what you are, belongs to being a human being who knows and understands what he or she's doing. You can't be left to yourself to suffer forever lost in your unique understanding, and another issue, do you wait for the world to be created for you, or you lead the way into a new creation? Where you are the center of everything, and you are not subjected, or isolated for the ideas you value. One where you are seen and understood exactly what you stand for, and valued as part of life.

You have to pass that world where you couldn't fit in or find yourself, where you were once common, and undeserving of life. Through your understanding you have then developed to a platform where you live as someone who knows and has mastered what they're doing, or represent, and that's the difference between the two worlds.

You once found yourself stuck in a universe where you felt isolated for what you are, and for everything that you know and understand, to a world where you're the main character, in that part of creation, and you cannot be discriminated or left out. You are the creator.

To everyone who lifted me during the writing of this book, it was my darkest moment, I had lost one of the most important people in my life, the only woman I have ever known who truly cared for all that I am.

I am lost without you...

Individualism

As you move through with life showing keen interest in being more, you could end up discovering something that needs your attention, which so many haven't known. Only that you as well have just begun in this present existence to study beyond and understand how to reach levels that so many haven't reached to. As you arrive at a certain area where you or no one has never been to, you could become consumed by that, and having to focus all the time can cause a lot of need to be alone, to analyze things better.

Finding that kind of unique talent can be worth more to a human being, even so, it doesn't mean you have to be isolated for the rest of your life, while you are busy exploring the world. Distancing yourself from those you meant to love does create a huge gap and emptiness that cannot be filled overnight, for most of your time, you will be feeling alone and far from people, and you can try to get used to being with someone, and you can't. You can only be able to commit to a person since that's necessary to be normal, in your heart you have reserved a space for your work and for the one that you will give in to at the end to be happy.

"I have never made peace, in my head and my heart there were so much that had been isolated and distant from each other. The fact that you believe in the need to live a certain life that no one understands creates a lot of loneliness leaving you feeling apart from human beings. As it is that part you cannot be able to share with anyone."

Living alone in your head, with the eagerness to hold on to something that you are, that you love so much, knowing it means everything to you, hanging in there, and waiting for that life to make sense. Depending on where you want to get to, you feel like you have lost, you begin to experience this poverty of spirit, that not even love can repair overnight. That sense of being abandoned creeping into your soul, with no one to care for, no pulse, to be standing at a certain place where you positively know what you doing, yet knowledge and precision has stretched out the horizon.

Is when you have faith that you will master what you doing, you do not only give what you can get back. You devote so much that you can't have again for the rest of your life, and when time becomes the ultimate test, you feel the loss of that part which you have given. For it is only when you know what you doing, that you can commit your time to pure understanding. You have passed the first level that you are a normal human being, and things do have an impact on you, and want everything as well. But you have taken a different path that leads to something which is your course, and that has stolen so much away from you.

These are some of the things we have given our lives to, and when you look at what you've become. At times you can't live with yourself if you never achieve success in that route. Then you have to get used to what you are, you have to pass through the decision to have known something else, and make peace with everything that you are now. To see a way to a better future, as you have sacrificed a life that would've offered you everything, and now you have taken a new passage to prosperity.

It could have been just a gift that you had, and you never wanted to be crucified for. Depending on how broad it will become part of life, you could suffer the strain of that coming to existence. It isn't easy, having to work at a certain level of understanding, so much could be determined by who, and where your idea will be used, and that can have a huge impact on how low your well-being can get to. For something that is essential for use and will become part of so many lives. It may become the toughest thing to understand or cope with, having to go down lower than you could bear.

You can be familiar with what you doing and how to do it precisely, in a level of understanding where you can't see the results of what you are now. So much becomes very confusing, in your head you have the perfect picture of how things will happen. For an idea that will interest so many out there, and you want to achieve that, while so much could be a sacrifice from the beginning to reach to it. Would you rather spend the rest of your life complaining of how you felt about things? No, you give the only strength you have, knowing everything depends on it to once again make sense.

You can disappear into it, when something that is part of your life is meant to attract a mass audience. Wherever it is, you enter into every gate and door of existence, and people with different characters, and personalities become the end-users, and you keep on descending with it. Then you know you have been consumed somewhere deeply, and for a very long time no one can ever pick you up. Remaining there with no heartbeat, you could be left to find yourself. This is where someone can arrive at, stuck, living with a need to adapt, and yes if you give in to the love you have for the world so much becomes better.

Unlike having to stop at a certain level, whereby you don't go beyond the normal expectation. You have given a limited commitment and only to a definite point, for something that might involve every human, without having to think twice about their engagement with that part of life. To some point you could feel helpless and defenseless to so much that there is, with everyone that uses your idea you become exhausted. Better that in love, you could try to come back, as the deeper the commitment you give to whatever you are could be reflected all over you.

It might be better when there are options, with different kinds of ideas to choose from. So what if you are involved in something that is the only idea that exists, there is nothing else, and there are no substitutes. Ask yourself how deeply taken can you be? How given away are you, with all these kind of lives that live out there, and above all that you could've done? This could be something that has pulled you somewhere so deep and your whole life might have disappeared from that.

The best thing to do is not always available, sometimes you can't even find true love from what you have become. So much could be difficult to understand having to deal with different types of people, who are meant to be part of your daily routines. If you had known them better, and how they live their lives, a lot could've been easy. For some are these kind of human beings that are very binding with everything that there is.

If only through determination you can pass those people who will be the users of your idea, you become better. As you start developing relationships that establishes bonds with them, and that can really help to recover from all the energy you have used inventing your life. When you fail to understand them, you keep losing yourself deeper into it, and remember that to do everything honestly is the only way.

Since you could figure out ways to overcome things not accordingly. As for your trustworthiness would've disappeared permanently, and the objectives which you suppose to carry would have vanished. As much as you wanted a certain thing to help human beings from, let it be of integrity, and not to expose them. People have a natural intuition that can never allow anything that has come to destroy their well-being into their lives. You must have found something of value to be or to represent your life.

I wondered how I began this life that had now swallowed me, torn apart, and left with nothing to live for. The thing is that it is so much you need to understand about human beings, some are difficult to deal with. While others have bonds that binds from deep within, and restrains you from being part of everything there is to live for. All that impacts badly on this person that you are, and takes away something essential to happiness. As no matter who you are, you are born from love. It continues to be the only thing that everybody wants in their lives, and if you cannot find a way to manifest your true love, you remain incomplete.

It isn't funny when your life is always on the line, and no amount of money can make that go away. When your mind is distant from everyone, so much become very difficult to live with. At the end, even the smallest achievement would have made a difference to find self-worthiness, and in most instances, there won't be any that comes easy. When responsibilities have consumed your youth and disappeared into adulthood, it's sad how things can happen. It just becomes one of those things that if you had known, you would choose to stay away from.

Now you are deep into it and you cannot go back, as you pass certain levels you're almost a grown-up. You had been alone for as long as you can remember, now it's time to break free. Prove to yourself you were not lost, and you didn't chase after shadows, to have always been involved in your own way of thinking.

One you had started as a young individual, and nothing made sense until you were almost an adult. The time you had spent isolated, almost as if your whole life things had been difficult, and you don't need to be told. You have witnessed that as you focused on the idea you wanted to live for, hoping that somehow you will have clarity. It would mean everything, and your freedom to once again become a human being.

To have pioneered your life as a young person, when so much has called you into focusing on what had been your true motivation. You become aware of who you are and the different parts of your understanding. On the first level of human perception, is where things are studied and we derive meaning from that. Then some things come naturally as part of our intelligence, which you cannot study from an institution, and if you never question yourself. You can live without ever knowing what it takes to become a different person or maybe a star.

To have questioned yourself, or know these kinds of things can challenge you with so much that exists, and if you never do enough to find what you are within that context of life, you can be left feeling empty. Only to look back and realize that nothing can be done for you, and you have been subjected from the world that is real, through lack of participation. Is when you haven't done anything or study what you are, you can fail to understand what more you had been. At the end you can give in to whatever there is available, while we all had our free will and power to be what we require.

The first thing you'll get to realize is that we all have died somewhere, where we are more to this life, and we are only left holding on to being ordinary human beings. To know isn't enough as well, you have to be prepared to do something that will reconnect you with yourself. It doesn't matter how you came to recognize that, better now that you've found what you can take pride in.

It could be late, however to participate will bring you closure, and with that, you'll come to acknowledge that you can be so much. If you learn to have value in everything that you are. Even though it might not be that worthy now, is somehow very meaningful to live for, and discovering how everyone is capable through determination.

Don't be surprised when you can't be what you use to be. Life can truly have a hold on everything that you are, through the path you have chosen, and you can try at many times to understand what you had been. Whereas you cannot be that person again, we never believe the road leads deeper into forever. It refuses to go back, and when your mind fails to adapt to all that you doing, it only brings you sadness.

So much has been combined to form everything that we see on a daily basis, and you can never know which is what. Once you get on it you are all taken, so little to you means too much to the world. Though is hard to hold on to it, you have to grow with it. You could have wanted to enjoy a lot about what you are, this life, and everything that you want to achieve. Only that our faith is tested on something that you cannot understand what it is.

If you never truly resemble that strong belief you can remain in the dark forever, and without a clue on what is happening around you. Only if you allow yourself to have that utmost faith in your knowledge, vision, and desire, that so much can become clearer as you go along. A lot is just meant to hold us back when you lack that spirit of loyalty in what you do. Especially when you are on that journey of your creativity, you can remain in the dark for a very long time.

It is something that you can never be able to share with someone, you just have to believe in it yourself. It becomes an individual concept that you alone must live with, it forms part of who you are inside. How all that you doing shapes the reality of what you know? Deep within your head is where everything has been happening and long existed before everyone knew. Is only us that knows what we have been struggling with, from the minute your life is down to the point where you can pick it up. Nobody ever understood what has been the hold in you.

It is more of an individual journey that you have to travel on your own. As is something that has never been easy to open up about to anyone, and you look at yourself and wonder. How will I be able to pass through this kind of a situation on my own? While it changes the reality of your life. Being isolated in your mind, alone in all that you doing, and that being the results of a particular thing which exists in you. Whereas you can't be able to confront so many with regard to it.

People never have problems like this, and what makes it difficult to share, is that we know exactly what went wrong inside our own lives. That's how much we understand and have faith in our present situation, and you cannot change, as there's love involved in it.

In your head you need to have worked so hard to arrive at a certain area where your mind produces exactly what you want to see, and how things must turn out. To be always pulling yourself to think thoroughly and deep, and never be ashamed of how long something took to understand.

When you work on that all the time, a lot about who you are changes and start channeling your life in the right direction, and that will justify the time you have spent alone. Trying to do things right and at the end of the day being able to say; "though it was challenging, I was always present in my head on thinking how to be doing so much that I call work, and therefore I have achieved success".

With no one to rely on you never feel things the way they are. You can be lost, and mostly you can try to remember where you came from with all these ideas that are meant to become the most important part of this life that we living. How you always have yourself to count on, as you are the only one who could be sure of what you have turned into. Though they might be unforgivable situations you have to face.

Leaning on yourself you begin to understand that people can make you feel like there's something which they can offer you, while there's none. You can only give that to who you are, and you thought individualism meant that you are alone, not being able to love. At the end you begin to realize that it means in your journey you are on your own, and no one cares or understands what is it that you going through, it becomes your only way of life.

Nobody knows another person, they can only try to be sympathetic, and you remain the one who is sure of your story. You let it be something that you are prepared to see, all over your life, and be happy with what you are, whether people understand or not, don't be stuck at the lowest level possible. Where you are as good as buried, by failing to accept yourself. That's what you become if you don't have knowledge of what you are. It can feel like a heavy load that you carrying, and that's how you begin to travel. Knowing that you cannot always be young, you have to let things happen as you grow forward, to mature is to rely on your intelligence.

Individualism to me meant so much, that you are a person with unique gifts and understanding. That you possess a special kind of talent, and not that you lack companionship in all that you doing. You are alone since you are enough, and you can achieve anything the way you are, even if there are people next to you. There won't be able to understand what you doing, and learning to trust ourselves as we have that much capabilities within to be the greatest.

Although life is designed to support our ordinary activities, the world is more of a platform for our easy routines. These lifestyles that we have towards our understanding alters the vibration of the universe to feel like we fighting against so much that exists. Hence our minds must strive to create a level for everything we know, through your knowledge you are able to design something which you can be able to rely on.

Even when situations try to be very depressing, you hold on to what you understand about life. Be aware of so much that you doing, though sometimes we could be wrong, even if you were right, it wouldn't become life overnight. You cannot know everything about all that has been from the beginning, the way is there to teach you as much as you require.

You could've been walking alone, not being sure of what you doing, and only building reliability on the fact that maybe this world could have been built strongly on the side of the truth. That law of honesty had been the pillar of life, and if you are influenced by being right you won't be lost forever. To feel abandoned can emerge from thinking that maybe there could be others who are meant to approve of what you doing. Still, know that to be on your own in everything that you do, is for you to unlock the true potential locked within, and no one outside yourself can free that individual who matters to you.

That's how we learn the importance of putting faith in our knowledge, you can try to look at the one next to you, thinking that maybe they can relate. Only to find that no one understands, people are living through their objectives, and you can feel very offended how things will constantly happen. When you experience something as if the world is against who you are, and then recall so much about what you know. Who does it serve, does it matter that it only means as much as you think to yourself, and no one is there to see the world through your eyes?

Situations are always trying to weaken someone every day when you travel in this path. On the other hand, can you allow yourself to be that weak? No, you have to find a way to overcome your weaknesses. Give your life an opportunity to become a very strong person through your understanding of what you love. If you are to succeed, only what you know about this world matters to the kind of individual that you will be, and when all has failed, does your knowledge sets you free?

Though you may want to be so much, there will be those you can't serve on your own time, and you have to allow a lot of things to come to pass. It only means that what you know now is not enough for everyone, those who are happy with your creativity could be what you need to save your life from the world that has died in you. It could be after a very long time when you no longer care, that so many could respond towards everything you love about this world.

Make peace and allow yourself to come back from what you know, what is it that you can do when you don't understand everything? Sometimes you mustn't care for all there is, the world that exists out there is stronger than what we are. The truth, in essence, does it matter, or it is only important when you're sure of what you doing? And if you not then nothing makes sense, honesty, this life, not any part of that serves a purpose. We questioned so much about who is above all that we are, you, the other guy, who has authority at the end?

The truth is significant when you reach to it, when you get to that part where you see what you doing. It doesn't matter who brings it to the table, sometimes is hard to understand and it only has meaning when you have arrived at that point. Whereby if the world doesn't agree with what you doing then so much will have to destruct. If you are betrayed then humanity has been misled. You are not leaning on people, you relying on something that is essential and is a core of everyone's life.

It is not much that we required, is just our truth or reality. Something that you believe must be seen or known, even if you have to be aggressive in resembling that part of you. Though situations may try to blindfold you, when you have seen you can't let it disappear into a world whereby it can never be life again.

If you want your part of understanding to become reality it has to be enough, it has to fit in somewhere, see where it's needed. There's common sense about this world that we all know exists, then there's the knowledge that we get from working hard. Which becomes life in the depth of the wisdom we have gained through the work we have dedicated our lives to. At the end, yes you cannot fail, if it aligns with humanity, even if is deep. If it is true then it will come to be, when there have been minor errors then someone can help you fix that.

Either way you cannot lose, people can try to close the gates and say that there is no way back or out, for what is worth the world cannot deceive you. It has to defend itself or else it destructs, and when it has been unable to maintain its honesty you must be able to identify the situation. What is the nature of the condition where it has failed to shield its well-being, what would have happened for reality not to matter? What manner of life would that have been, and when it has been weak in protecting itself can you understand what it entails for you to do?

You will understand a lot about life in the path that you traveling, you cannot be stuck in a situation where things become so impossible to handle. Even when so much has died somewhere so deep, and the truth has turned to being insignificant to be lived. If you stop seeking after it, then you didn't want it. If you don't get to the end then you never wanted to understand the whole part of reality, you are the one who controls your destiny.

Everything does get to a point where it becomes defenseless, especially in the path that we find ourselves traveling. Which is where our faith has been cultivated, and whatever matters to you, will come back to form your life. You could have lived to chase after shadows in so much, but an honest purpose will establish your understanding where you matter, and when you arrive at the end. You realize that you have formed your truth, through whatever you embrace about yourself, and now everything makes sense since you want it to.

You work tirelessly every day to arrive at a certain place, where you understand that so much would mean everything to you. If things never make any sense you won't ever have peace, and if it does create meaning would you handle the truth about what you need out of life? As that's how things develops, it begins from nothing. If you resemble courage, it grows into something more meaningful, and if you truly want it your well-being starts to depend on it. You have to keep going until you arrive at that place where everything becomes love for the world, the secret is to be prepared for all that will come to be.

You could have seen yourself as if you don't belong from the ideas you possess, and why is it so important to have your goals manifested? Is what has now become a purpose meant to change your life for the better, and you have nothing else to live for, except that you will come to love that about you.

Maybe you are not satisfied with who you were, and the whole world will once again make everything matter. As for what you had been living wasn't enough, you feel like you have something more to offer. You are a gift to humanity, and you must be cherished, you can't work to destroy that. You embrace it, as is good you have in your heart.

You couldn't fight to deceive the world, you feel more like part of it. You believe in the well-being of humanity, and you can't kill it where you have seen it. You hold it tenderly with love, you don't want to look at it as an opportunity. However an obligation to serve, or maybe you just brought too much caring into this life, and everything that you had been doing is now based on that. As we all have our share of reality, maybe yours is to care.

So live to resemble that kind of human being that you dream of becoming in the world. Not a lot can have that opportunity to understand what they are, and what it means to so many. If you feel like you are well equipped for this life, then focus your attention on being the best that there can ever be. It could have been something that you never knew you can explore through your intellectual capacity. You just became content since you dedicated your whole attention to serving it, and it responded well to that.

Chapter One

Obscure Vision

Though we cannot see where we are headed, we keep on moving hoping some truth will reveal itself towards the goal we have set for ourselves. You never really know why you have to keep going, it could be that in the meantime you cannot remain in one place.

There has to be somewhere you need to be, being alone in all that you doing. Stuck in your head, so bad you only wish the outside world can understand what you doing, and no one can. You on your own, Isolated by the concept that exists in your mind, and worse you have been trying to break through for a very long time.

What can make you linger in darkness, is being a first timer in the world of creativity. Eagerly awaiting to break out of the system of commonest through your knowledge, the way things can take longer to understand. Remaining there in between times praying for salvation, wishing that maybe you knew, or you have been there, and you have never been there, this is the first time. Longing for the experience, only to find that you have none, you just have the will, and you not even sure if what you doing makes sense.

You can get lost in so many stages, and not that you don't know where you going, or what you doing. Just to be alone and need to trust yourself that whatever you doing is right, and it must produce results. How vulnerable you can be, almost as if you can have faith on someone. Whereas you on your own, and worse needing to have confidence in your ideas even when you're required to be very patient with everything that you know.

Lingering in between times, knowing you could either have got it right or maybe slightly wrong. Yet the whole scenario is more accurate than incorrect, and yes you could be victimized by every stage of your understanding. So much can find you in different situations of life, and that part might interpret your knowledge in its way.

Part of us knows that we will be successful, and you hold on to that, whether the world understands or not. Even when you can't get used to it any more since you have given so much of whom you are to seeing something happens. While you could have lived for a very long time down there hoping that things can change along the way, and it has been like that.

It has always been you, stuck in situations that you don't know how to break out of, and how you became accustomed to that. In a way that you no longer wish anything on yourself, and along the way you have learned that to have a unique vision doesn't have to be confused with being single, isolation or negligence. Is just that concepts need to be thought of thoroughly, and you cannot put your whole life in your hands if you haven't worked hard enough to trust in your capabilities.

Know that if this is to become your only way of life, then it must be reliable, and that must give you strength to overlook so much that is happening in the world around you. Focus on what needs you to pay attention to, you never really know why the need for that.

It could be that you cannot be found playing if your fate lies within your understanding, you wasting your own time, and your chances of success. It might require one to take things very serious from as early as possible, though you could have been lost at some point, now you need to create a winning mentality.

This is a stage in your life where you must be careful, so much could be opposing the person that you are, and you never really know what you fighting. Only that a lot depends on your understanding if you are to succeed, if you don't you fail your well-being. It is always this journey's that we have towards our creation that feels like we against something.

I had traveled in isolation, or maybe both, and individualism, pushed by the world to be in that kind of situation, and on my own trying to get things right. So much felt like it could be enough when you want it to, and you can wish for things to make sense when you require them to, and it doesn't. It could only be good for you, not for everyone, you need to see everything beyond your world of creativity, and take center stage.

I was tired of believing that someone will come and make my life better, I had matured deeply through the love I had inside for what I am, and I needed to do something about it. I was just by myself living the only life I have ever chosen, and without a doubt, I had been so happy to have witnessed this kind of understanding.

Though to thinking different, there can never be any pride and justification, you are justified by the end, when you see what you have devoted yourself to, become successful. You could be someone struggling with finding a way to break through into a new world created by your knowledge.

Going into this kind of life, you never really know what can challenge you, and you don't need to hate or hold grudges with regard to anything that opposes your ideas. You just keep on believing and looking for a path forward, and when something does at some point stand in your route. You want to know how bad it can influence your entire knowledge and understanding. As so much does affect us and the way we do things, and you feel like everything is at large and against all that you know. Imagine being new in the world, and only to have a huge thing standing in your way, you feel like is over.

How weak that can make you feel, you cannot lie to yourself, when things don't go well we all wish we were different people. Living our favorite lives, and that can happen with anyone. Is only in you that you get to understand what so many have gone through, when is someone's life you just see the results of who they are. You never really get to know how they traveled to that place that represents the end of their journey, and why should you give it up without seeing the outcome of your work, and what it was.

If only it was simple then everyone would have made it, you can let yourself be fooled that there is jealousy and hatred, and you can only agree to that when you still lack understanding. If you have completely done your part, you go through that spirit of negativity into a new world, where you are really convinced that no one can stand right in front of you when you are truly capable of doing what you know.

You grew the belief that everything that stands in front of you, is there since you are not ready now for a new world to come alive in you. If you have worked and you have gone beyond the normal understanding. You break barriers with your knowledge, and you appear in the next chapter which is meant to be your reality. The obscure vision disappears, and you become a new person who lives the life they truly desire.

Obscure vision is the difference between reality and dreams, you can have visions and ambitions about a certain world. No matter how close you can get to making that a reality, if nothing is definite, then you are still imagining things, and anything can break your heart. You don't want to be found lingering in that state of mind, you want to see yourself living the actual life, which you had been longing for.

Is like a glass that separates you from your true desires, although to have that hunger is sometimes better than being stuck in darkness. However, you will not have peace since you want the true meaning of what you yearning for, to be completely lost on the other hand cannot be justified by anything.

The significance for all your activities beyond what people can understand, is that you're being formed by something so magnificent in the world of knowledge. Is creating you in that isolated space, and it doesn't mean you will never live again, you will be given a chance to be human and an opportunity to love as well.

Yet that formation is not only meant for one human being to see, or be attracted to you, is for the whole world to understand what you are underneath. You embody your ideas into reality for everyone to bear witness that quality of working tirelessly create your happiness. You become the wheel that drives the creation forward into a new and a brighter future.

How can you ever doubt that period in your life to be worth something beautiful at the end. Is when you standing in one place that you cannot see what you doing, that you can almost think of giving up. When a day becomes longer than one can bear, or understands, a week gets filled with so much that needs to be done. Meanwhile you don't know where to put the blame for all the sadness that you feel inside, and it pushes you to question the only thing that has led you to the exact place where you are right now.

How a dream can leads to your failure? Actually no, visions and ambitions don't fail, we just don't get it right from the beginning, and they die with us.

Only to envy a certain world can mislead you at one point, you can wake up back to that reality you once were in. On the other hand to be carrying your own goals knowing that you do as much as it is required of you, can never disappoint. All these concepts that are left for us to travel through are mostly things that are not studied by institutions, hence they're difficult to grasp without being truly determined.

If it was to be studied then we would have got it right from the beginning. Imagine how broad the world is with things that human beings got to understand on their own, without having to study, and that is individualism. A person has become an institution for their ambitions and they don't need to be taught in that regard.

So you get to recognize the part whereby you again has become that for yourself. Learning everything you need to know alone, and you can do something amazing with that. You can strive to be the best and truly stand out, we don't have to know the same thing. With the world of creativity we remain as separate people representing our unique, and different thoughts to what the world has come to see so far.

You mustn't blame so much on yourself, as things don't go right when you want them to. You can hope that some truth relevant to what the world requires will come to exists. When you have seen the power of determination in making anything a reality, you will understand why the need to perfect ourselves. Nothing fails to come to light, everything passes through us when is ready, and we let it reach where it will fit in.

We let it see the light when is complete, and so that should be what we always hope for. That the dream will pass through everything, and that is very important to prepare for. As you might see the part of life that poses threats to you, and become very afraid to focus on your progress. Now if you have what it takes for someone, you will beforehand get ready for whatever it takes.

You cannot escape reality, you will be formed by every day that you go through. Until you get to know that I am good at what I do, and be confident by learning how to stand apart from the rest of the world that you will see out there. You become so strong in manifesting your dreams, the things that we usually encounter along the way is what we need to drive ourselves to success.

Mostly we fear that period in our lives, where you cannot materialize from what you know, and that's what questions our faith towards the life that we have chosen to live. As people who seek understanding of what to do with what they have turn out to be.

You can be found in that period of your life, deep in spirit seeking for a way forward, and thus mostly the point between our own lives and the world. At the border of our understanding, from your reality to the global community. You might be questioned so much, and yes a lot stand to examine the intentions that we have. Our motives towards everything that we represent, and by resembling faith in your work, when you have done things accordingly, you cannot be refused.

You cannot be denied an opportunity to see the formation of your creativity, whatever stands to question your integrity towards the life you want cannot win. The battle is within getting things right, it comes as a process of understanding. Your work won't leave you until it is perfect for the world, and when it becomes ready, it will proceed to the next level. That will prepare it for the other process which is not part of your life, and again you've got to identify how far you must push it, that's your role in it?

You must choose which part of the world you want to participate in, and how you want to approach things with everything that you know. You can either have two mind-sets about the world and a lot that you doing, you can know so much, or you can be level headed.

While some things don't bring out the best in us as human beings, they keep taking more of who we are. The right thing to do, even though it might not be simply, could be to pay attention to what brings out the greatness in you as a person, a quality of your life where you progressive.

Unlike doing something that doesn't allow you to grow since it could be about so much out there, and that is likely what we face; two equivalent worlds. Only that one feels better than the other, as it doesn't allow you to put your fate in your hands, or develop your skills. You keep on standing in one place fighting for recognition, at the end there's none.

So find a place in your life that allows you to grow and focus on that even though it seeks your whole understanding, pay attention and when you begin to find meaning. You will feel that now your efforts are directed to the part where you are valued, and to be sure you're on the right path, you can choose from two personalities.

You can either be a specialist or general, and that can give you exactly what you want out of your ambitions, and not to be afraid embracing one of these ideas. Which could be more advantageous, you cannot develop in so many areas at the same time, you have to excel somewhere and be productive from that.

Then being a specialist could be the best thing to be, than generalizing your concepts, you find something that you know how to do until it manifests what you need. As you could have known so much and maybe it didn't work out, now you feel a lot like a failure in everything that you doing. Yes you can reach the end with all that you understand, and life could be better with what you wanted. Still, it might take a very long time before things take a direction by which it seeks to travel.

Now when you specialize you can focus on the area of your life where you're good at, and maybe even in that part where you know what you doing. Don't do so much that will leave you feeling dehydrated, be involved in what you best at, which will bring more out of you. With the rest you can keep growing with time, not to grow unproductive.

Focus on growing efficiently, and it says so much about the kind of people that we are, when you know that here is where I'm good at, keep doing that. It raises the level of your commitment and the standard of your work, to just pay attention to the best part of your entire being. Unlike when you generalize concepts, your attention could turn out to take advantage of your whole understanding, and fail to see the part where you must excel in what you do. Is not all the time where you need to do everything on your own.

You cannot stand to judge yourself, find others who specialize in the next part to evaluate you, there are a lot of situations where this kind of thing can occur. You could be a singer, or maybe a writer, you can sing and produce on your own. Complete the process and finish your work, however that didn't bring out the best of your abilities. You will work tirelessly to the end of your understanding trying to prove your capabilities.

So if you can write or fine tune your melody and make sure everything is perfect, and then get someone to look into it. When you're done and complete with everything find another one who can effectively distribute that for you. It would make a lot of sense, and saves you time to be able to focus on the next task you have, you don't know which part of your work people will love the most. Everybody that comes in, gives it a different look and feel than when you just keep moving on with it on your own.

It could be the same with everything that we engage in, when you're serious about what you doing, you don't have to wander in the dark. You can prepare your work and focus on that only so that it can be magnificently beautiful, and find others who specializes on the next thing, which is what you cannot do for yourself.

Life becomes easy like that, and your creative understanding turns to be a joy when you approach things from that angle. Like that you are not entirely in an obscure situation, you living in the light, if you don't use a different approach you fail the whole process.

You might disappoint yourself where you know exactly how to do things right, the next person in line takes you higher than you had been, don't go down low. Move up with the stages, and better your understanding. You could be great at the foundation, yet you may drop your own efforts when you reach the end, which is entirely wrong about everything. You wasted good and precious energy devoted in doing a certain thing. You too as a person could become something magnificent if you allow that spirit of being a specialist in your work and life.

If you just focus on a specific aspect of a project, you develop more every day, and that opens up a space to be formed by the work you do. You move with the process of growth, since these kinds of activities we engage in can have you remaining behind forever. If you never reach a solution to what you doing, you will not pass to the next stage, if you can just stick to your passion, you find a way to progress even when it's rather impossible.

Dwelling in that love becomes the most incredible way to grow into what you seek to understand, and be precise in choosing a way to live your dreams. Don't take it lightly, know that some could be the best, raise your head and see the outside world it does exist. Do not shelter yourself in lack of reasoning and think that reality will pity your life to have what you desire, that won't help you to win.

Rise into the real world with good focus in all that you doing, it does exist in you as a human being, and from that little dedication you can be fortunate. Once you get that chance be prepared to be the best, and sometimes accept it when something has failed, or when you have missed the point.

You can be holding on to what no longer serve a purpose, your objectives must be clear as time will not always be on your side. To have a unique talent that you specialize on speeds up our lives to manifest our desires, like double-edged sword your mind cuts through everything, and who can hold you back when you sharp like that.

Though so much can have you feeling like you living under pressure, when you have to dedicate yourself to doing things right, and there's something good about the love we resemble. We grow to the next stage, unlike when you live at a level where you comfortable, you're being unproductive, you get used to be fed everything. Creativity is about growth, we have entered an era in humanity where we refuse to mature, we keep holding on to things that are not who we are. Except that, even in situations like that you can achieve a great progress.

A perfect understanding of everything that you doing, it was not wrong to have had things done for us, besides that, we don't have to refuse who we are. We are people destined for the greater good, and that can only come to life, if you focus on something that you know. You don't have to grow through hardships, you can mature through hard work and commitment, what you come to understand will lead you somewhere beautiful at the end.

We are not forced to understand things that are no longer necessary for us to advance to the future. From that we can motivate ourselves to acknowledge what is right and required of us to stand apart. We can even do better than the last generation, by applying our knowledge and perception about tomorrow, regardless of so much holding us back. You can allow the present to form you into a better place by making use of all that you have available.

Though it doesn't happen in one day, you hope that in the future you will need it the most, and that's when it will be important. Since life cannot be something you refuse to move through. So when you're in it, if you there to become so much, and now that you have no other objective except for this one. We can say that it can never manifest at your first encounter.

For what is worth throughout your whole journey you would have gained knowledge to accomplish everything that you desire out of being this person. With time you can experience so much coming to existence. It will not be about what you like, is what you are capable of doing, and being focused on that is determination.

If you are ambitious to sacrifice everything for that sake, you pass one stage of life and move to the next, and if you let that be what drives. You can get as far as possible, though we are never equipped for this kind of knowledge. You can achieve it by being aggressive in resembling what you believe in, and we are meant to see the way through that. Your focus makes your dreams becomes clear, and is not at the end where everything will be bright, you shine the light even where is dark.

Chapter Two

Reflection of Beauty

It doesn't matter who you are, you can be anyone, and by continuously doing things that are not necessary we can reach where the world is defenseless. It could become vulnerable to every attack there is, so much that we do does add an impact or ruin the beauty that the universe resembles.

However our work of creativity with love can be able to heal that part and with time it can begin to blossom. Although it might not happen in one day, by tirelessly working through it, somehow it does change. Every effort will not go unnoticed, it becomes easy to understand when one has invested their life and energy in doing something great.

We all get to play our part, when you have felt the need to do something special, and when you don't get that chance. You feel denied an opportunity to be a human being easily, so when you do have that break, don't forget how unlikely it was for you to reach there. As everybody could be a risk to this Divine creation, and you too had been that kind of a threat. So try maybe once to prove that the world had been wrong about you, and do right, don't live up to such expectations.

The beauty about creation is what we all possess, you could have missed that side of your life, as you've never learned to channel your energy in the right direction. If you can look away from everything happening in your surroundings. You can realize that part of yourself come to being, and so much is that we never thought that we can make a difference and a good impact.

Except that, either ways exist, you can ruin everything that is great out there or you can do something amazing, we are that much. The thing is to care, if you cherish the idea, now that you wanted to be of that world, regardless of how difficult the way could be, you can become a blessing to so many.

If you have chosen that you are here to do some good, that is what will come to manifest without a doubt. The rest of what can make you feel unworthy, is the part where you never learned anything about creation, and you are still not there yet. So much about your life is formed by your past, and some kind of ideas where you were not sure of what you doing.

If you can move out of that old age into a new platform, you get to understand that dreams can destroy so much that we are. Only to rebuild all that we love in a better place, you just need to arrive at that level. Walk a mile in your new shoes, to realize that become true.

The goal can be something hard and difficult to achieve at times, moving forward with life. It might become impossible to break free from what people have created, and for a person who is eager to establish an idea that will influence most human beings.

You might be surprised at how the world is, looking at things from a perspective of being a good part of humanity, or someone who wants to shape reality as we know it. You could feel very offended by the works of those who live without care of what impact they're making with their creations, and what that could do to everything we see daily.

We all form part of the universe, and you will never know how powerful you are without ever trying to involve yourself in it. You need to have prepared to do some good, as it is that which creates the way forward, whatever we do answers so much towards creation.

With good intentions, everything just becomes relevant to what exists out there, as you can never know how the future will turn out. Only that If you feel motivated to do what you love, it will align with what human beings are. As that's what we are at the end, people formed by the same thing and one big reality.

You could find yourself stuck, and as one become desperate to move on with life. You might begin to develop some ideas which are not necessary for someone to apply in dealing with human beings. Not that the way isn't there, or maybe no one cares, many could be concerned.

It could be that for now your fate lies in your hands and you might need to work beyond a level that is acceptable. You never think you have it in you, we are pushed to that horizon, it becomes a must to develop your knowledge and capabilities, until you fully rely on your understanding.

You could feel very strained, working towards perfecting yourself to be a star of your intelligence. Your work, talent, and capabilities are for you to break free, and push your mind out of that comfort zone into a region of what you desire. That is how you approach things and everything that you doing, which will say so much about how you reach that place, where you see what you are.

Through the situations you had to pass through, you get to know who you really are on the inside, or maybe you could have been wrong about so many. They did try their best, it could be that to be your pillar of strength, changes one into something they're not.

So much may not be how we have perceived it to be, and to attain it could be at a very high price, and how it can affect your whole life. It can come with a lot of difficulties and changes, and you could begin to realize that this life is not meant for everyone.

Is for those who are willing to go through everything, hence human beings cannot be there to support you all the way. When is something common about us people, someone might be able to play a very important role. Now that you are the only one within that society, who refuses to see things from a normal perspective, it just become worse.

Many can fail to understand, and you on your own, and there's hardly anyone with the exact assistance that you require. You become lonely and isolated that you can suffer the loss of hope. While you need to rise above the standard and see life beyond what a lot can perceive. You are your refugee, no one can help you realize the potential you have inside.

At times you are pushed to be very creative to break out of that self-limiting mentality and witness your understanding reaching that point of transformation. Through those efforts you transcend into the next level, since it couldn't exist, if you didn't see it. Now that you certain of it and it lives within you, there's no other option except for you to find it.

The way is there, that you know very well you might need to travel on your own. Even if it means that for some time, you walk out of your comfort zone just to make things happen. We sometimes become so glued to our old age perspective even when it requires for you to step out of that space where you're stuck, and make way for something to be possible.

For if you don't nurture the idea, you could experience a lifetime of difficulties. You mother the thoughts until they see the way, you support all your efforts, like you would with your children.

Ideas require that much parenting, we bring forth all that we are until it becomes life. Just like a child that you raise until fully grown, so that one day they can return the favor when you no longer can. We always set realistic goals, and a positive side of you always knows that beside so much that you can refuse to be part of, it is possible.

You wouldn't want to involve yourself in something that you know very well is impossible to achieve. You know you can accomplish it, and you just become selective of ways in which you need to apply to realize that.

The goal can affect all that you regard very high, and you can lose a lot of what you value with your whole life, including love. So much can suffer the strain of that when you don't fully understand what you need to do, and we find ourselves lost. Even where we have so much to live for, we become too compromised to see the way. As no one can relate to what we are, and we refuse to associate that with the present situation.

How our lives are now dependent on that succeeding, when something instantly becomes the driver of everything that you are. Deep within it turns into a song that you sing until you feel that poverty of yearning for success taking over your understanding.

When the present certainly doesn't give you enough to live for, and the future becomes the only place where you are destined for all that is life and happiness. When it happens, so much that has always been the problem that tied you down to nothing disappears, and you will have deliverance. From the experience of this harsh reality of how you lost everything that you once were.

Even though it was you who felt the need to live without it for some time. The goal can deceive you, and can lead you to a place where love and so much is no longer there. As we walk out of a lot that is meaningful, to have what we truly desire.

When you are focused on the beauty part of life, which at times you can wonder what it could be, love can pass you. Yet we are led to that place by a lot that we go through or which isn't right, it might happen that something could have been wrong, not entirely.

It could be that to let go of the only thing that you were may lead to so much being ruined. Imagine one error leading to destroying so much that you value, and it happens all the time that not everything is too impossible to bear. That we can refuse to ever settle at that area, is just that some things are better when they're perfect.

We are not perfectionists, it could be that we can't live with being inadequate and that's how we decide to live so much that we were behind, and we have few places to be in life. The next place you might need to rebuild all that you are, could require you to be very creative in terms of understanding, and now that we didn't grow up there. You may be forced to work until you find yourself, and everything that comes with success, and to reach for that beauty part that represents a new beginning could be very consuming.

At times you must ask yourself what is beauty as the magnitude of it has no limit. It could be what you hold close to your heart, and we have different possessions that we are very affectionate of. Some keep careers as part of their greatest achievements, some embraces love as their measure of success.

Which if they don't find it within their current situations they can look for it everywhere they can reach to have it again. So much can die or disappear where you have known things, and you might need to search for it, and as hard as it could be to find quality in life.

You might need to travel spiritually to that place where you derive that value for something as precious as life itself, and that may not be an easy task to achieve. We look away from so much at hand to find meaning in the future. Tomorrow is what we designing with our present thoughts, and we make sure to create some good as everything we do will not only impact in the whole world without impacting back to our own lives. So is ourselves that we creating, to witness what we hold come to be, and harness a lot of greatness in society.

The objective that we must allow to drive us regardless of situations could be to preserve life and not to destroy it, with our harsh mentality. As we become desperate to see what we want, and it happens all the time when you can't have what you desire that you just decide to ruin everything that is love around you. Which is wrong of someone seeking to do some good in the world, when you understand something that you cannot look away from, make sure it is based in doing well.

Since we do get the rewards for all that we do well, we harness a lot of greatness so that we can make a difference with it, and everlasting prosperity begins with a true foundation. If you strive to pave a way for admirable work, then you must have set-out with an excellent groundwork.

Do not ruin the beginning, and expect the end to be something else, you want to make sure that the beauty that you seek to see is exactly how you began your life. Everything comes down to how we started, through a perfect establishment you have a concrete success, as is something that doesn't repeatedly need to be fixed.

Regardless of how you feel questioned, as so much can stand against us, and if you don't have faith in a good foundation and new beginnings. You wouldn't make a difference, even in the previous life you had, you cannot get away with lack of goodwill. As we are not the only ones that live out there, and always striving to find a way to be the best, and that could stand to judge your worthiness.

Without righteousness your abilities are compromised, and when you challenged where you not completely sure of what you doing. You become threatened so much like your world is coming to an end. As you know the reality we exist in embraces competition, and you can't take it out of whatever it is that is creative about people.

As long as there are human beings that participate in that area of understanding, there will always be a need to stand apart, and within it, there is standing firm. So make sure that when you realize that people have brought all that they are, that you bring your best. Reflect your uniqueness in a good way, which says a lot about your work and how well established you are. Represent something that is life and speaks for so many that are what you reaching out to, is what you will always be remembered for.

The need to stand apart, cannot be overlooked for whatever reason there could be, you can't take that out of any work. Is lack of rivalry that destroys the beauty in everything people engage in, and when you feel like something could be a challenge in your way. Ask yourself, if is not about the fact that you have failed to do your part, as that cannot be ignored. So don't always take your side even when it doesn't fit right, embrace the central theme of all that we do.

Don't be left confused and frustrated by that kind of situation when all that you need is to see the angle where you are very devoted to exciting and involved with people. If it wasn't about being greater than the other there wouldn't be any reason. Always remember that being a star is about perfection, and you're questioned if you are at those heights of understanding.

So strive to reach and pass people's expectations and enter a new level of excellence with your work, is the only key that unlocks every door deep into our fears. We could accuse the world of being biased of what we do, while is you who failed to surpass so many who stand on the same platform with you.

Fix your mind in doing something until you reach that point where you excel, there's no need to even fear what the world could be. What pushes one to be afraid is when you haven't done what is required of you. Your knowledge, understanding, as well as expertise must be able to set you free. All you require to invent your life must be independently based on what you're capable of doing for yourself.

Though you will never go into this kind of life, knowing everything completely, and until then you not enough for the journey that you traveling. So much on the way depends on your knowledge, you want to win and for you to do that, you must have striven for it. There are a lot of things which were not actually in our minds as we approach this platform.

Except that when you arrive at the end, there could be a lot based on that, so see the way to the finish line. Since you can never know what lies ahead, all that you need could be there only needing you to be focused.

So do not only strive to get there, reach for it and make yourself heard big time, since it doesn't matter when you arrived. People don't need to know or understand who you are and where you coming from, they want to see the performance.

So mature as young as you could be, or as old as you are, don't relax as the next person might do better than that, and that's the kind of creativity we must embrace. Beauty where is loud and clear, it wouldn't mean much if we didn't do it in a way that is meant to last, and that's what improves our world to become more wonderful.

Is when you feel the need to be better than the last generation, as the founder of a certain idea you hold the beauty and the future in your heart. All that you have ever wanted lies within you, but do you have what it takes to resemble the wonder that you seek to show the world.

You might have never been very strong in carrying yourself forth, still, your vision mustn't change or fail you. Though you may require someone to help you with something that you cannot do for yourself, you must be the big part pushing your faith to that place where you're eager to be.

You might lack the experience, beside that we all know when something is good, and when it has been done right. So don't go easy on yourself, be hard at times for that part of your life to come and do something amazing. Which you know stands out, and to acknowledge when you have failed. So is not about who you are or expecting the world to go soft on you, even though you might feel like you have tried. Maybe to try may not be enough, and you cannot say is who you are and expect everyone to understand.

Come closer and upfront, take center stage where you know that here you are your best. So if you find it very hard to bring that out of yourself, you might need something that truly inspires you. Even though is hard to discover that kind of inspiration in ourselves, be persistent until your mind settles in.

Though that can leave you feeling vulnerable to time when you not sure of what you doing, if you ever discover that gift of something more about your life. It will defend you against everything that might seek to embarrass you, and you get to understand that nobody hates who you are, people fall in love with the beauty of our work.

As painful as it might be to stretch our horizon, you need to try; can there be a way that what you do can be done better? If not, there is only one route, which is to work and wait, hoping that tomorrow will be productive than today was, as it does happen to the best of us.

Standing there you could be wondering, how am I going to break through the wall into the other side of the world where life is formed by creative intelligence? Even if there is lack of knowledge and understanding that can restrain you from entering into those gates where you know you now belong.

Thus when you're required to push yourself to pass through that with everything it takes to be a star. You could have thought that it would be easy, that you will just do something or want to be someone and the next day when you wake up so much would have come to be.

Accept that it doesn't happen that way, you need to open that door of love and creativity, that exist deep in your sub consciousness where all your capabilities lie, and admire who you are. As no two people can ever be motivated by the same thing, so you find your center and what works for you. Something which enables you to move forward, since you cannot remain behind forever.

When things are not where you require them to be, you might feel the strain and the pain of that life coming to be, and we constantly question ourselves, on how to push into that world where we seek to be born. We embody our knowledge, understanding, and capabilities, and with that, we are able to see ourselves through, and everyone is capable of doing that. The magic comes to exist when is really what you seek, even when you have to sacrifice what you are right now or risk it all to see that happening.

Always remember, that you never lived until you take a chance on your dreams or achieve what you love, and it won't always be like that. You risk from here to there, after that is life all the way, what living would mean if you haven't risked anything. So think it over again, what it truly means to you, as the passion you resemble might be what you need to push yourself until you enter at that level. Where you see what you desire come to reality, for if you don't give that last energy it will not come to exist.

Live with confidence in what you do, knowing that it will redeem your life at the end. You wouldn't take a path that you know won't give you what you need, as the more you devote yourself to doing everything that you love. Your understanding begins to be dependent on that, and for so much to make sense once again you must do better.

It could have taken longer than expected, and you might have remained behind than it has been necessary. A lot seems to be now taking a lifetime, and the time for what you require could have come to pass. Is just that you mustn't let it disappear with you, and without ever getting that fulfillment.

Dignify your soul, as it will never rest until it sees what it stands for, the thing is that so much become formed inside, and it might need you to do what you love which is what you stand for. We are here as human beings meant to carry our inner desires to life, and it doesn't matter if it exists within if you cannot carry it through. So make sure you have given yourself to what you worth, which you are not forced to continuously be every day, and move forward with it.

You will not believe that if you don't pass certain levels of understanding, then you will always remain the same. So make sure you see challenges as a path to more, and do it for all the right reasons, as beauty means so much to human beings. So do it for life, love, and everyone who cares about everything that you are. As they as well are depending on you finishing what you are perfectly to see the wonder you hold underneath.

A lot before is life can only make sense to us, only that you must allow everyone to be happy with the end of your journey. Let people see the good you hold in your heart, and don't rest until is done, give it all the required energy and dedication that it needs. It might require for you to have dedicated yourself so much, and believe a little bit more. Not for the reason of what you are in the present, for everything, yesterday, today, and tomorrow, all make-up for the person that you are, and you're used to that by now.

Bury a lot that you don't need of yourself and begin to focus on the positives. Obviously, you do have so much that you don't like about you, given that somewhere along the way, you not settled, and you still require improving. So that is just the part where we don't love everything with regard to ourselves. As for now the journey continues and you're meant to write new history concerning your own life, so be creative, and create a lot that you will cherish regarding you.

That is how so much goes, we fall in love with something special within us, so do your part, as this is not about all that you have ever known, is for a greater future. You make it happen beyond what so many can understand with regard to you. Create wonders in every turn that you take, in your life, love, career, and in everything that you come into contact with. Since we do touch plenty as we go on, including lives out there, so be a blessing, and magnify beauty.

Chapter Three

Wonder of Life

Apart from standing there trying to understand things better, we tend to criticize a lot of what forms the reality that we see daily. The present could turn out not to be what we love about ourselves, is just that you don't have to discriminate everything that is going on out there. As there could be a certain behaviour that you feel necessary for life.

You could have your point of view on things, which led towards your approach to whatever feels right for you. As different as you are, you don't have to be negative about all that lives outside your world. So many are only trying their best to cope with so much the way it is. They don't feel the need to escape the present to find meaning in the future, and we as well must learn to live with that.

They stood firm and try to understand what the present can offer, by resembling a very strong character in accepting and learning what to do with what they have become. They could have done the same to overlook so much which isn't working for them, and hope that maybe one day a perfect world that lives in their heads will come to exists. At the end you realize, it doesn't happen like that, it takes a miracle to witness a different reality which could offer us exactly what we want out of life, and to live at some point is enough.

It happens most of the time that a certain way of living can emerge that is just there to ruin lives, and it could be motivated by anything, leadership, or whatever it is capable of influencing the reality of what we see daily. You can be confused, so much ending up walking away from life and everything, only to become a human being through your intelligence.

Before we are formed by our understanding, we are sometimes created by what the world is, and regardless of our differences, no two people are the same, and a lot could change at some point as one seeks for recognition and you can fail to adjust to the changes in situations.

A new world can emerge meant to take away everything that you have ever known, only to look back and realize that it did not just ruin your life as a person. It has affected everything, from your love, family, and a lot that you value, and since you are not ready to give up. You still feel so much need to be human you have to stand again, now that you're being questioned of what you know. Can you pick yourself up, and find that very strong and unique individual that you are? Given that whatever pushes you out of what has been created, must be a powerful force, to have had such an effect on you as a human being.

What you have to understand is that it might not have affected everyone. It only impacted on you and the majority are fine with the way things are, and they are free to move on with their lives. Plenty of times it happens that we didn't prepare ourselves for the worse. You just saw an exciting world and aligned with it, and when a need for change arises you fail to adjust.

Right when you think things can never be too bad, you're confused and nothing makes sense any more. You can't find value in the present, and it is so unfortunate that reality doesn't care deeply enough, for us to remember what we use to be. Even if you can apply patience, don't hope for anything better tomorrow.

When you have failed to see beauty in the present you don't fall close, you drop too far into the depth of misunderstanding. Worse you cannot assemble enough energy to fight back to reality and with determination to find happiness, you can't even get the strength to be part of life. You can work night and day, there's just no passing something like that overnight.

It takes a lot to push back to the world, especially by passing through that which is directly opposing what you currently are. The best thing to do is not always available, you can try to look around. Yet there could be so much that you don't understand, or maybe you looking right straight into things, look aside to avoid direct contact.

Even if you have ideas which you believe are the best, carry them with you, don't permanently isolate yourself from all that exists, or which is life out there. So much can have a hold on you, so bad that you won't ever know how to win the fight back to reality so early.

Our efforts or everything that we understand must fit into a certain system of all that is creating the world in this present day, that's what pulls the energy to be human to us. When you have failed to find courage today, it is hard to hope that tomorrow you can end up being the person you want to be. You are not built for war, yours could be to find a way to make a living from whatever is available.

To live is to adjust and adapt to the current situations, you don't know what serves us life, and how big it is. So don't be in denial of the present thinking that maybe one day you will be prepared for all that challenges you, things do oppose who we are. However, it is wrong to look away, even in relationships, when you need to find real, meaningful love, you could be required to do the same. People who are worthy of being loved are those who have been trying to understand things and they have decided to fit themselves to whatever the world is.

So you understand the part where love cannot come to you, or nothing comes to us, we go out there to find life, relationships, and everything that is part of it. Is never certain that you will reach all of it along the way, it could be that if you stay in one place the sure thing is that you will not gain anything. Either way, the solution is to go out there to search for something meaningful and worthwhile.

You cannot lock yourself in complete change and isolation you have to take part in something, or so much that exists. Decide what works for you, even when situations are hard as hell, make a room for whatever you can reach for, it can never be what we always hope for all the time. Sometimes there will come a world that isn't comfortable for us, and you might need to pass through that to get to where life is good.

It all doesn't feel right, but if you don't do it, you might never find any meaning to the end, at times is not that the world has changed. We fear the future and we refuse to move on, that we rather remain constant and do nothing with what we have become, and that is what holds us back. Is not that we cannot make it on our own, we can, only that you need to live a little. Is not sad what you will discover, you can gain deep or derive meaningful insight into things. Even though your part could be on the other side, you have to walk through that uncomfortable side of reality into a brighter future.

We don't know what could be the price for holding on to our ideas, or maybe is what will allow life to be full of happiness at the end. It might be that adjusting to a different view on things is living as well, it is good that you will find embodied in your newer perspective. You go out there to be human, even as a child in this spiritual world. You must learn to make a baby's first step, that's how you become a valuable person.

If you just stay down there you cripple your soul, learn to interact and be content of yourself within that community where you now exist. Even if you don't know what to get from it, don't remain at the bottom forever. Reach for the value of what you are, it will attach you to something worthy in the meantime.

You have to continuously feed on whatever is available, and not to be laid back forever, is that part of your life which you need the most to be human so hold on to it. Is there, though it might feel uncomfortable, it is life, is where you are now a person. We are in a field where everyone has to occupy their positions, and you cannot say that you playing when you not in it with your whole heart.

So get inside and be in the game, and not to be without a purpose that keeps you alive daily, make your presence count. The thing is that you missing out on the best that there is, and you holding yourself back so bad, and for a very long time you won't matter. Everything will give up on you, as we are meant to grow where we focus.

Things add up to one another, and you don't have to miss a thing; not that what you thinking or doing doesn't matter, it does. You just need to do it in a way that isn't completely isolating yourself, from all that exists or which is life currently. Yes we have dreams, as well as visions, and we want to do something amazing with what we are.

Still you don't have to stay back forever, even the ambition can take longer to manifest as alone you cannot make a difference. You need an input of people out there, and they are there to help pass these stages of misunderstanding which you didn't hope will be easy to go through.

We are not meant to know so much or handle things well all the time, or maybe someone could be that for you, not everything or everyone opposes you. So don't go against it, rotate with the ball called the world and see where you fit in, or are likely to be appreciated for so much and what you are.

Creativity can lead you somewhere wonderful, and your mind cannot be completely dead as it is, if you just go out there you can find life. Though at times we are trapped by situations that we must pass through, chances are that if you go with the flow you are likely to make it out successfully.

We don't know why we are this guilty of everything we seek to be. Maybe apart from what we want, there is life outside, which needs to be celebrated, that you must pay attention to. You not undermining the capabilities that exist inside yourself as human beings, you adjusting to situations and being part of life. You making something of the present, loving the world, and becoming part of it, by moving through it with confidence.

Unlike what we do to ourselves at times by walking away from everything, as if we did predict what the future holds. Life could need us to hold on to so much, there's always a way to be happy, you don't have to lie to yourself. Feeling like you're stuck, even with the goal in your mind be involved, and live the moment.

We are never completely stuck, whatever you think is a problem, is better than choosing to be alone, or going through life on your own. If you cannot make use of the present, even the future might be the same. Everything is always right here with us, you just have to like it, enjoy it, and make something of it. Do not go far, as the results will always be similar, constantly look around to find yourself, don't be outplayed by avoiding where you are.

You might even think of changing places hoping that it is worthy, whereas the value is always in the moment and around us. You just have to know what to do, and not to be comfortable in your quest to achieve your ambitions. Dreams do come true yes, while not living as well, you might miss out in so much that is vital and worth more than just love itself.

You cannot overlook as much as we have to be human for, and the need to have been prepared for it, is always a very crucial part of finding happiness. What if you never groomed yourself for the present moment? You only realize now the need to be happy, and whatever you do goes around that, and regardless of how much you search for your worth. You can't find anything to celebrate about this life, or maybe you can never be ready to live fully, so if you can make peace with everything you have.

You can begin to witness the marvelous ways we have at our disposal, and don't think that it won't be essential to have ambitions. It will always be necessary to have dreams, since it does not only exist on the outside. Is what you are on the inside, and that gives you the power to aim at the next level, and to increase on what you have. As the wonder can grow if you give it a chance, whatever we embrace keeps on emerging, and forming as our new lives.

On the contrary if you decide to live right now, you not only living for a minor intent, you're meant for everything, the present, the future, as well as love. Is hard struggling to keep up with things as you come from behind, the whole thing is about not losing that much. Is about gaining more as you move forward with life, while holding on the need to keep growing.

Sooner or later there will come a situation whereby all that you thought justifies the time you took apart won't matter, and when you think that what you doing serves the purpose of humanity. You discover that you are only serving your ambitions, or goals, and the world won't care about that part, things would have changed.

So before you get ahead of yourself with thinking and dreaming big, you need to be on the same surface with everyone. By celebrating beauty in everything and all that exists, as hard as it can be to adjust to situations don't look away. As you may never have enough knowledge to come back to reality. To reach at that point where you're important might happen, as you could be thinking of life where it matters the most to humanity. Given the fact that regardless of what happens outside, everything has its place, and you could find where your ideas fits in.

Irrespective of whether you aiming high or low at life and so much, rotate with the universe until you find yourself where you matter. As we do serve a purpose to some reality, and remember that not everything out there is against a human being. Something worthwhile to be living for could come to exist, and you have to find what it is.

So choose your path carefully, as there will be where you don't amount to so much, and where you're important as well, and as soon as you gear up and begin to live at your best now. You will come to witness that truth or reality you desire most coming to be, as part of what you're correct about whatever you doing.

Although as part of our creativity we could be right about certain things, only to ourselves, and wrong about so much, as we lack exposure to reality. Don't permanently refuse to be common somewhere, our world is a fantastic place to live in, and you can find yourself living an imaginary life, created through your thoughts. As you lack people to help you see things from a different perspective.

Though some things are just meant for you, and you can achieve them if you want to. As nothing is standing in your way, only if you can get up, put everything behind and work for it. Even when situations are made hard to understand, you begin to grow forward. Not everything is for everyone, and yours could be that life which will come to exist through your efforts.

Imagine how long it would take to matter if you insist on believing in your own ideas, as you can't be everything yourself, and it isn't bad. Yet there's something that you might not be aware of, the fact that you will need approval to be a human being so full of life. Once you disconnect, you will need to reconnect again, why not avoid all these complications that we encounter along the way, you don't have to go through so much.

You can live it all and still be what you want to be, is just part of celebrating your uniqueness. How can you allow yourself to be isolated from life? Especially in this modern society where almost everything has advanced. Is not that ideas don't exist in human beings, they're there, and they matter the most, it could be that no one seems to care about that any more.

We are living in an ignorant age as if there's no need for an idea that will complement reality as we have come to know things. Perhaps it might happen that within you as an individual you decide to pursue your own goals, you know where it will fit in, and you have faith so much in everything that you doing. That you see exactly what you referring to, unfortunately there's no one to invest their resources, and you have to risk all that you are. Since you cannot look away from it, as you believe in it, in such a way that it has become the only thing that you want to see manifested.

The thing is our ideas can hold us back, or deny us an opportunity to be happy from the reality we want to see happening. How do you work around everything and remain normal in society? As something has got to give for the person that you are, and the time you have given to your desires, we are not meant to do whatever we like our own way.

Though you could be from a world that hasn't given you anything for who you are, and you never mattered through the objectives given to so many, and is so ironic. From deep within somehow we are the ones that worked away from everything. It becomes true and evident that you can't go in there with something in your head that seeks a way to live. That could be able to hold you back, or refuse for you to find a place to settle.

You can become a human being with the gift inside, is us that live ourselves behind, we refuse to look and see the love that exists in everything, that is worth being celebrated in the present. To find happiness now is to be a good part of existence, how can you look away from such a beautiful thing called life, you have to accept something, don't reject it all.

To look away simply means that what matters to you doesn't exist in the meantime, it will only come to be in the future. Nothing guarantees happiness tomorrow, though we must look ahead, to avoid surprises, we also need to hold on to what we have today, how can you let creation pass you by.

So if you want to achieve a certain thing, it won't come and give you happiness tomorrow or love wouldn't come to exist in the future through that. It was always here with you all the time, you just didn't care, and maybe you had blindfolded yourself thinking that something else will give in to what you want. However, we always have what we are, we just live in denial trying to expand our territory, while everything you need is right here with you.

A lot about human beings is that we want things on our terms, and not that life wasn't there, it is forever here with us all the time. You can't have something that you not, you have been coming with it for a very long time. If you are meant for a certain thing it has always been yours, don't look away, or refuse to pay attention. There is so much about being focused that matters to what you currently need, it makes things happen. For those who work for this life, you had it from the beginning, you just didn't know how to have it, the way you wanted it.

Even when something could've been yours you can fail to see, as your focus always runs away from so much we have now. Be a force when moving towards achieving that goal, and the dream. Is the attitude that you wear daily that will be exactly what you get out there, don't undermine the enthusiasm you have for life, as you can never satisfy the hunger for existence.

What you need is right now, where we are, to enjoy what you love about everything. If you believe in the present, you will find yourself in situations you have been stuck for a long time, hoping for a miracle to come and change your life, whereas it has always been free.

The beauty that we seek is always what we have now. How can you make use of it, to expand it, into a meaningful thing for everyone to understand, and find a way to realize what you have and how to be happy with it? As you not completely alone and lonely, love could be there you just haven't opened your heart to it, we not entirely abandoned, and our world shattered.

If you need true love, hold on to what you have first, is there, you just need to pull it, and not running away from the moment, saying there's no possibility of happiness. How can tomorrow be worthy, when you couldn't see a way to be content today.

We must have a way to embrace these conditions, by appreciating so much in the situations we find ourselves in, maybe is not precisely what we want, or hoped for. You wouldn't see the value in it until you saw how important it is, it might not be everything that you understand yes. At times is to question what to do with it, and device a way to grow to the next stage. Of all that you could look away from, there's love, how can you not be pleased with someone who has and is willing to give themselves and their hearts to you.

We all don't know why so much could be wrong at times, and why are we not happy with where we are, and want something else. Maybe we are not satisfied, is true you know that this is not what I love, and you see a way to work it out. As bad as you know everything out there could be very harsh and there's no room for humanity's problems, and lack of understanding, you want to squeeze in some of your true desires.

Somehow you must give so much for everything to come alive, and you're prepared for it, the thing is our lives could be fine. Is just that we constantly are required to make adjustments here and there, and the need to change things. Given that is not everyone who's happy with where they are, and you could be pushed to make those major life decisions. More like abandoning what you are, you refuse to understand and believe this is who you are. You feel more deserving and full of potential for a better future, and a motivation has arisen, and you must answer the call.

Is so much that has been designed to waste our time, and not that you won't reach your goals passing through that, you will. Is just that someone can invent something they had been working on for a long period, and as they get a chance to implement that. Only to find that it doesn't necessarily align with who you are, it just messes everything you have ever known.

Still you don't let that be the ruin of man, even if is your own life that became infected, don't remain behind forever. You can take some time off just to clear your head, but be always content with all that is happening. We are not meant for everything, yes, so dare to face every day, as bad as it can be.

You let what you know doesn't deserve your love and attention fall out, only that you don't need to allow everything to pass through you as if you have predicted what tomorrow might be. The future could keep worsening, at the end is not the world you running away from, is yourself and everyone who cares about you that you neglecting.

You lost who you are going to the core of life, when you allowed so much to slip by. We require that much of ourselves, and intact, as you don't know what you fighting. You could be against your self-esteem, so don't be discouraged by that much, as the universe is not predictable.

No one can do or be exactly what you require, you are that deep within you, so don't be sad, circle your dreams, and visions. You let the center in you be love giving to the whole world, and to what you long to see. Right where you are, you begin today to look for beauty where you've lost touch with it, and it can be everything that you need right now. While living with a point of view and a progressive mind, and you can go further.

You can define all that is life for you, and without a doubt witness it come to exist, what is it that you want where you are that you cannot have. It could be that you not looking hard enough, if you can look intensely, you surely will find the solution to whatever you desiring.

You could have spent years not knowing that within the environment you at, you have the same capabilities to do something worthwhile, and if you can search thoroughly. You will discover the beauty and the wonder of how splendid your life is. You just have to love the world we live in today, and open your heart and do it in a way that resembles caring, so look no further, right where you are, is as good as it gets.

Chapter Four

The Work of Heavens

What do you expect from this life, as you wake up in the morning, to the minute you go to sleep, what could it be that you require the world to do for you? We live in uncertain times, yet a lot of human beings still believe there's justice, and it's true, maybe is there for those who deserve. When they have done their part, and as you look outside, there is no reason for someone to fail. Can you really blame the universe or anyone for your failure, as well as for the things that never worked out the way they were supposed to?

At what point do we actually stop believing in what we know how to do, and put our faith on the reality that there is something that we serve, which is supposed to deliver us, when all that we love doing seems to be delaying? That if not by the aid of that thing which is greater than we are, there wouldn't be any easy way out.

As it does happen that you've done everything you could and so much still isn't getting any easier, and you don't know what to do. As you believe there has to be something more, and only through that, regardless of how you have done things, if is not by its power, then it can never happen.

Are there any miracles or something more that can come and save us when the time is right, or anything that the world can do for us, when you least expect it? Knowing that in every way possible, is not through the work you have done, as you not winning and you don't know why. There seems to be an external force that has now become part of the scene, and as much as you would like to argue, you feel that is now out of your capabilities. While the will to see that happen keeps growing more and more, and that is regardless of who you are and where you coming from.

Deep inside you feel that you cannot do it by yourself, and you wish for that supernatural thing, which by some power can help you succeed. As you not the person you were anymore, and the way has been a little hard and longer than expected to reach where you want. You live with the believe that something unexpected which you can't do for yourself can rescue you. Is true, part of what we desire the most are things we don't have the ability to make happen, and you can really appreciate some help.

Success comes from within, however there's an external factor which is supposed to deliver that to you. As it wouldn't happen if there was nothing or anyone who can give that to you openly, and that's how people go through the experience which they feel is not fair to who they are.

That something was supposed to be there, to make things happen as they wish, and as that doesn't come to life as they have hoped. They begin to suffer the setback of their life's work being delayed. From all that is available out there as part of what we interact with, there need to be a reliable entity, which is there to help ease situations a little bit.

We are not meant to be involved in everything on our own, whatever it is that we do needs someone to work with, and for that to produce monetary results must be loved. It doesn't matter what it is that you doing, it could be an idea, product, or any form of artistic work that inspires you, requires a recipient. Someone who serves as a receiver, and gives value to what you have done, and that person not only loves what you did, also feels obliged to compensate you for it.

Is being creative for everyone to love what we do enough to open the gates for us, is it all that it takes to earn a living from our work of understanding? The situation turns to feel like it needs some sort of an assistance to govern our relationships with so much that we interact with against everything, jealousy, hatred, and discrimination.

Is it always the case that when something is very interesting, then there must be someone who not only loves it? Feels the need to acquire it, in order for them to own that particular thing. It's so unfortunate that many are feeling denied an opportunity to be what they're passionate about easily, as we do find our place in people's lives at the end.

Does being a first timer makes it a lot harder than it is, given the fact that maybe on your second time around, you would have passed that point where you're in need of so much? At the beginning everything feels like a mountain to climb, there is no easy end to something and how much one keeps pleading for them to be accepted. Is not what you can do for yourself, which is the problem, is what you want another to aid you with that turns to be so difficult to achieve.

Maybe if we knew how to do everything for ourselves, so much about our lives could have been better, can a religion have anything to do with it? The fact that you believe in a certain way which you have based all that you do, as it comes down to faith. Can there be a clear route that you need to approach what you doing, in order to understand how to succeed?

Something which is there to make the path you traveling easy to cope with, and you only wish you know what it is that you must be. As a lot of people are more neutral to what they believe in. Is it that now when you're in your journey to find more you need to be very decisive of what you rely on?

In our quest to reach for our desires all we have to hold on to is our faith, we become so obliged to hang on our beliefs. Though we base more of what we do in our capabilities, we at times find ourselves pushed to the edge of understanding by everything that we seek to be. When what you know seems to have reached a dead end, can you still carry yourself forth?

How would you have known that along the way you will need to believe in something more than what you doing, and when you didn't invite God at the beginning of your life before this journeys began, why the need to call upon Him now? Can it make sense to change along the way and base everything that you are on the Creator?

How would you justify what you have become as someone who has been working towards a goal which never became any easier as days goes by? Can you say that faith you picked up along the way, and that God turn out to be what you needed as you went on? As at times is hard to be baseless, you need to base all that you are in something more, and you cannot believe in a certain thing which is not concrete. For you to be sure that you have a solid foundation you must put your reliability somewhere, what we trust on is supposed to be bigger than what we are.

An entity out of our control and which is there to deliver the greatest strength from all that we cannot do for ourselves. Is where you surrender what you are, and you know that you can't go beyond the level which you have given, and holding on to nothing you become vain, and darkness takes over your life.

What makes us linger there, losing who we are to so much that being without a belief is, what pulled the person that you are closer to divinity? Knowing that it just started with an idea, and is what there was to it, there was nothing more, you were just a person only that along the way things became unbearable that you needed your whole spirituality to deal with it.

Deep inside you confess that you began your work without any faith, you were just a baseless human being living through your own will. A lot that you became was how you felt pushed to give in a little more than you currently are. Can you say that regardless of the need you feel to be faithful, is not God you trust on, is your work?

What brings that out of an individual, the obligation to push themselves to give all that they are to what they want to see? You honestly understand that without a genuine belief in what you seek to be, here you have arrived at a point in your life where so much that you are right now has led to nothing.

You acknowledge that you're being faithful, and that what you feeling is something more, yet it is not in the heavens. Then where is it all based, can the believe we have in ourselves be enough? As faith is supposed to be bigger than what we are, and if you trust in your own knowledge and understanding, knowing that it came through you, then you rely in yourself. Is the work we engage in, better than what we are, if our work is greater than what we are, what in us produces that sense of devotion to come and transform when the need to perform our duties arises?

You could have the talent and the courage to be the one that is determined all the way. Still, when you decide to put faith in yourself, you actually believe that you are greater than you can admit. To take so much that you are and say that is not by the work of God, is by the will you have inside, that you really agree that you are the greatest. Could there be something that we seek to bring to life by engaging in this kind of activities? Which is what you are that is very reserved through the discipline you have within, that only comes to being when you begin to engage in what you do.

More like an idol that your creativity has become, and is taking shape with every day that you engage in it. It becomes the perfect creation that understands all that you are, and through it you're able to base so much that you do. Maybe you can put your faith in your work when it has been done great, that it is the only thing to live for. Does it matter how much expertise we have applied for it to be greater than everything we have ever known?

Maybe when a work of art has been done well and accurate, it can allow you to put your faith on it, and just like that you have your pillar of strength. As that's what we seek out of life, something that is more than what we are, that can let you to rest your head on it, if maybe that is not enough could we need to seek for more. That regardless of the fact that our understanding is where we have put our trust on, is our ultimate guide. Which feels so good beyond what your creativity can do for you, and it becomes relevant to rely on when so much feels like has turned its back on you.

As you can be able to kneel down, and plea for a way forward. It could be a point in your life where you feel questioned by so much that nothing makes any sense, and you could seek for it, just to hang in there. You can be threatened by all that exist out there, now that you only have your knowledge. You become shaken by what you are, against what the world is, and there's that need to hold on to something else, and is not like your weak. Is just that without an entity to rely on you wouldn't survive a day, your mind would slip into a part of existence which is not who you are.

That turns to be one of the most important factors that we need to consider very well, the fact that faith guides us through the path that we traveling. It helps us to persevere, and to resemble virtues that are deep within, which no matter what you are, you wouldn't reach for, and you can't do it.

Regardless of how you force yourself, it becomes the magic that we have inside. How would you have known that the journey will become so complicated that you will require more than what you can give alone? Or we can say that we are never that intelligent to understand the path we must travel, including the purpose of the way of life.

Part of what we do is just there to serve as a reminder of what we are on the inside, and we mature through it and take responsibilities for all our actions. As we stray out of the way and travel whichever path we find suitable for us, and when something isn't working, now we turn to look for a route which could be available out there. Faith is not only important when you need to hold on to it, through the journey you have chosen as a form of participation throughout the whole world, is also needed for you to be content as well.

Perhaps now that we living within the only way we have ever chosen, we've come to realize that is a must to have faith. Maybe, or regardless of the path taken we wouldn't make it far without it in us. It could be that traveling in this route of life we come to realize that we need all that we are. Is not only important when you want to succeed or understand how to cope with the person you have become.

It has always been elementary, it could be that nothing has ever questioned your worthiness towards anything that you doing, and it is needed whether good or bad. Comes that time where is the only thing that is standing in your path and you cannot move forward except through it.

Along the way we must decide which route to take, what do you believe in? Do you have faith in doing good that will help in creating and rebuilding all that is life, or you are about destroying everything that you see? Our beliefs are part of the gate we must walk through, and is not only meant for you or someone traveling this journey to understanding, is for everyone. We need to fulfill that calling, you could have avoided it forever, and now is time to accept that you're required to embody it.

As leaving that behind could affect everything that we are, from deep within our hearts in order to find something we could be happy about. There must be someone who comes and give themselves to us, even though we live in a world that you can hardly trust a human being. We expect them to love us honestly, regardless of what could be in line, and without pride, just to surrender freely. That being one of those things that without consideration of where you come from, and where you are, you don't want to be penalized for.

Though true love is hard to find, now with a strong belief in our hearts, we stand a good chance to actually attain the happiness that we seek, it doesn't matter what you believe in. There has to be someone that is made for the way you living, what is it that is within being faithful that is just meant for you to have everything that you desire most, joy, love, and your goals.

Meanwhile if you are true to whatever you doing and you cannot have what you need, ask yourself, is our faith divided? Where we are able to see that this is for life and this is for loving that special person, and at times we might require to carry one so that you can understand clearly what you doing, or all to have whatever you deserve.

With faith it could be regardless of where you are, that you need to resemble it for whatever you doing. You must work to cultivate it in you so that it is able to give you all that you seek within that period in your life. You cannot say that you faithful when inside you not truly complete, you let yourself be driven by that towards so much that you desire, and is meant for everything that you love. Without it you can hate who you are, that you not moving onwards the way you're meant to, knowing that what could be the problem lies in that part where you must focus spiritually.

When is it that you actually admit to yourself that here you are wrong to be living without something genuine for the life you deserve. Is not like you not focus, you are, is just that you're doing a certain thing, which is without that deep enthusiasm for you to have it at some point in the future. At times faith is holding on to what you want to achieve in a way that you can never go back. When certainly there is no way forward, you know that deep inside you must go on to have whatever it is that you find necessary.

There is that place where you know you need to arrive at, with your whole heart, and no matter what other ways promises to have. You can never make peace without ever getting there, and that's the reason for carrying yourself with utmost faith than ever. You are not strong for one thing to come to life, you resemble your beliefs for everything that you desire, including love. If you don't do it you might never have that opportunity to live well, and the way is meant to be, you become devoted for all that you long for.

When the path you have identified being the only way to have everything you want, you work for it to become life. You wait for it to make sense so that you can have the love, and the money, as well as everything that you really need out of whatever you are destined for. Is when deep inside you carrying a certain idea and regardless of how situations are, you refuse to give up as is your only way to happiness. You hold on to it, and explore all the different opportunities that exist until you find what really works for you.

To be living without that part of your life that you must build reliability on, at some point is to turn your back on something that truly holds the only key to your innermost and deepest desires. To just look away knowing that at the end you could have been the happiest person ever, and pressure became too much that you couldn't handle it very well. Now is just meant for you to live with feeling sorry, how can you give up something that you know you were meant to be, which deep inside was for you to find everything that you truly worth?

In the path of understanding where our faith is tested we put up with so much that is not life for us. So that we can have that little ambition which might not mean much now that you haven't achieved it, only that if you can reach for it, is everything to live for. The answer at the end to all our troubles, becomes the goal that we're meant for, and along the way we don't struggle we mature for it. Now that it has become the kind of life that we don't really need to be shown the way, just a route that you designed for yourself.

To remain true to what you doing does work at the end, when you have lived honestly through it. No matter how reluctant situations may be, something does give in at some point, as well as the love that we desire. Is just that at times we find it hard to realize what to do in the meantime, and when you need to carry on with your life normally, you could find it difficult to understand what to do. As so much along the way is unbearable and you could be left with nothing except to give in, that's when you require that extra energy to carry you through everything.

Is how you distinguish yourself from the rest by believing more, and whatever you have faith on, at the end does become the answer to all that you looking for. Even if it doesn't seem to justify what we put up with, as we go through so much and without expecting it, years have passed. Everything has disappeared and you remaining with nothing to live for except that goal, and so much does question what we've been doing and the reason for being part of it. Looking back the way no longer exist, and ahead there is no reasonable purpose to hold on to, and you have to find your grip.

The work of heavens becomes the rescue back to being human, when all that you doing has no place in the world. Except that it has turned to be what ruins your life, when you cannot find where so much that you are is meaningful. As everything has lost its significance, as well as in people's lives. Only to come and exist when you insist on hanging in there to resemble what you really mean, explaining and referring to it with faith.

Through that spiritual commitment it was able to create peace within your life, and it became recognized as you live the virtues. As it could've been what you needed from the beginning, since you were meant to come across mountains that you needed to climb with your beliefs.

No matter how determine you are, for someone who has been traveling a journey of creativity you might be very tired to keep on going. That is exactly when you feel like there should be something that you serving, which is merciful. As this world has shown you no love, and you know is the result of the path you've been on, though we refuse to serve, we choose to answer to our own will. So comes that time where you need to work for that thing, where all our efforts are recognized.

Regardless of how you feel inside you might need to prove that you are not the loser you have resembled by being focused on your own goals. As being a genius is put to the test, though you're sure of what you doing reality checks on us, just to be certain you're still content of yourself.

As not many can understand the world through our perspective before all has materialized, as it is first and only important to you, and it can never go away. Unless it has brought you results, and the crown for everything that you doing will follow with the joy that life will give you when you see what you are come alive.

Although it would have never been possible until you showed that much faith, who would have guessed that you as well will live to be remembered for the good you have created? As it is the hour of glory which reflects that you as well will be celebrated, and as your life will be praised others will be there to share in the joy with you. Now you have a reason to be proud of yourself, and what you've created. As either one of the two has made it possible, whichever it is, God or your work coming to life and manifesting through its own will.

Your work coming to life can close all the gaps that exists, as it finds a way to breath into the world of man where is hard to belong. By becoming a reality even when it could've been difficult, and you have seen countless human beings making it every day, thinking it's easy, maybe not or for you. Only that you experienced it when it became a reality in you, for as much as you wanted which never had a place could now have find where it's meant to be in people's lives. If it didn't feel like anything then it doesn't mean a thing, if it feels like the whole world was against you, then it means everything.

Again something that cannot be overlooked, that it required for you to be good, whether it was an idol or not. It needed to be worthy of putting your faith on, and that is regardless of the fact that is not war out there, so if there was a battle of Gods, you would need a very strong one. Then you realize that part of everything which being precise in doing things and making sure you stand out means, and with genuine belief it would make sense above all that is life out there, and to you as well.

So if it was God who make all things possible, what would it say about you, now that you have never resembled any faith towards Him from the beginning of time? You just remained behind with nothing to show for, as the Creator too, needs that much from you. How would you feel if you were tasked with presenting something that you know is not well done? Beside that it would be good for you that the quest to something that you truly desire which the way never became easy, taught you so much and changed you for the better.

A journey to finding yourself became the way to find all that being an individual means, and you have built a very tough character. One which is not a failure, and you might have never witnessed that much of success. Now it has come to you in the most unexpected way possible, and you are able to face yourself. As you know that you stand for something that is truly meaningful, and though you almost were ready to give everything up. You hanged in there since you believe in an entity greater than you are.

Chapter Five

Revelation of Faith

You could have been coming with it for a long time, and for what is worth you have never witnessed any form of success from doing whatever you fell in love with. You keep sinking deep into the dark, you know you're meant for more, and you believe that things do come to life at some point. Although you might need to deepen your understanding in whatever you do, and what's evident about so much is that you will not only learn one thing. You will understand just about everything you require to be the best.

As you head out there to become what you deserve, and focused on the need to express yourself, you do admit that what matters is success, and you fix your eyes on that. Even though it might happen that you not as good as you want to be in every area that you choose to be part of, or in that talent you seek to represent. At times you wonder how to improve on that as you strive to build a deserving character, which not only sees an opportunity to be successful, one that is truly determined to stand out.

When traveling on a path of being a greater individual, you become familiar with so much that can try to stand in your way. While some things happen since is who you are and what you represent, some are just obstacles in the way we have chosen to participate. It can occur to anyone who is usually focused on becoming something more. Hence is always there to test the most common attribute towards the life we have chosen to live.

There will be parts of life where you know that without a doubt, and regardless of what you go through you good at, and that gives you the strength to hang in there, and that so much happens as you are a human being. It becomes important to keep in mind that, whatever led you out there must always remain the main priority, and be confident that if you wanted something, is what you will get.

You came through a certain path which could have failed you, or maybe you just wanted more out of this world, still, be happy it was able to carry you to where you wanted to be. Now you have found a new purpose, and you can no longer go back to the person you were.

So much that you see and what you know is officially formed by that part of yourself, and going through this life feels unnatural. If you somehow are prepared for it and not lazy to stretch your horizon or to act upon your thoughts. You can discover something good about it, is what you will come to achieve as you resemble true commitment.

You could have been living a life that never gave you a thing for the person that you are, and regardless of how much you involve yourself. You keep losing more of who you are, part of you continues to be consumed every day, and you wonder how you became associated with it. If something is meant to reward you for all your efforts, it will be doing so right from the very start, giving back as you begin to engage in it. You can discover a way like that, which is meant for your entire well-being, and it keeps nurturing and taking care of your every need to become a better productive person.

So you learn to be grateful, to keep getting more out of it, and not to blame yourself if you once engaged in something that never served you a purpose or lead you towards a prosperous direction. Talent is hard to reach for, if you ever find something that works for you, show determination, have the courage not to ever go back.

So many times is that we have options, we give faith that is not enough for us to know that we can never be what we were. Give love to what you choose to be in a way that it becomes the only thing that matters, don't find yourself stuck in between two lives.

Though is a side of you that is young and new, so far it has given you more for all that you know. If you can remain confident in it, and refuse to let go, for the first time you would have found where you belong. As depressing as it could be, look around if people have made a living through, it so can you. Is not every day where we lead our ideas into a part of existence where human beings have never been.

Is just out of the ordinary, into a place where is about talent and you are there to showcase yours as well. A level of understanding where you're reminded not to undermine yourself as your creativity matters, and is what will say so much about you as well, so you learn to communicate with it.

It could be a life where you need to constantly show how much you value about what you doing. Though we came through differently and we regret so much about the people that we are, and you could have groomed yourself in your own way, and is only that human beings are not the same.

As we come from unique circumstances, and we all could use some differentiation. What you are has prepared you for everything that exists and opportunities in the future, and we are those kind of individuals. Well prepared, thoroughly ready and know how to do so much with the little that we have, and we take it from there.

It's a world that focuses on the positive about you, it doesn't see any negative side from what you are. It circles everything with love and puts it on the spotlight, so don't cry for the person whom you use to be. Embrace this individual that you are right now, show some appreciation, give faith to this beautiful thing that you have become, and you can never know why it turns out to be marvelous.

You would have paid your price, and this was the greatest you had to pay, as being born in this level is the most expensive thing that you would have ever achieved. The fact that is a side of our lives that sees no wrong to what we are.

Though you might have never been appreciated, here we are given the best value for our talents, and maybe is about time we get what we deserve. Which is exactly what we want, to be recognized for all that we good at, and you don't always know what pushes one to have a desire for a life that is extraordinary. It could be the knowledge that you possess, you could have something important to share.

As unique as we are and from different worlds to represent some essential part of reality which is hard to find in an ordinary world. What could be straining you is that you have not find a place where you fit in, or where you are known for what you do, and not that everyone doesn't care, you might not have arrived where you seek to be.

Yes we care so much about the people that we love, on the other hand, the world has turn out to be everything to live for, or sometimes cold, and now for a very long time is about yourself and what you want out of it. If you don't reach that goal, you're not useful to anyone except that you will keep taking more out of their lives, and to go back is not to show them true love either.

So if you keep going, and disappear into it until you find your place. You resembling how much you hold them closer to your heart, and that's how you will find a room to accommodate them. At times it doesn't matter what you live behind, what matters is that you will have what you need, and everybody will be happy about it.

To care, is always at the center of our hearts, only that we could have changed, we no longer of the same formation, and what forms us now is the world in spirit, then allow it a chance to run its course. Let that part of creation creates you, it's just scary to start as you don't know what the next stage might turn you into. So don't be afraid of yourself, you are infinite possibilities that lie deep in your soul, and you are never the same thing, it's a world full of surprises.

Whenever you engage in your activities, you transform, so don't feel discouraged about every day having to wake up to working hard, you becoming a new person. Sometimes you might feel afraid and depressed to go on with what you're meant to do, yet you don't know what the next level of engagement will have for you.

So whenever is time to put yesterday behind and accept today, feel courageous about it, and give yourself to it once and for all. The best thing about this part, is that it will always not be where we are born, we are from an ordinary world. We work our way up to the stars, whoever has made it, is for themselves to be what they needed to be.

So you continuously work hard to push yourself forth to a better place, the more you engage, the bigger your platform expands. So by refusing to labor you remain standing there, and you could be from a world where you've witnessed hatred, and maybe a lot of negativity as well. That you don't hope for anything at all, so bad that it has affected your self-esteem.

Only that if you still feel the need to change your life and be something good. You must remember for the rest of your existence, that this is not the part of creation where you've lost everything you valued. This is a side of our lives that never takes anything from a human being, is here where we are given back what we love. So act upon it, give in to it permanently without hesitation.

A place where your dreams and hopes are valued and with no need to hold you back from achieving it. As it has always been evident that you cannot seek to be something you not, then there's no reason why you shouldn't be given a free platform to have that. Whatever you want to be, is what has always been part of you, so it matters that much to you and for you to have it.

Regardless of the situations we encounter where we feel denied to be what we want easily. So play your role as not everything out there is against the person that you are, and it will forever be like that where a side of your life will always depend on you.

Life can deny you so much if you are not where you need to be, and that's what you must be running away from. A world that seeks to devour you, that has given you nothing for what you are, and awaken in your new level of existence created by your creativity. As you don't know what might be waiting ahead, love could have been hard to find where you use to be human, or maybe you have been searching for it in all the wrong places.

Now it's time to come back to reality with a very strong attitude, a human being that sees everything differently and positively, or perhaps you could've been denied joy at some point, now you can have true everlasting happiness.

We tend to think less about ourselves, and that we don't deserve as much as the universe is ready to give. Except that you need to come back with it, understand what this kind of devotion means. An opportunity to have the best, if you can conceive, or see what this life can do for a human being.

Then you cannot deny yourself what you really love, and you don't have to be afraid, so run away from that disappointing world. As bad as it could be, seeking to devour your soul, don't embrace it, for it has given you nothing for who you are, it just keeps on taking everything you have.

Don't find yourself holding on to something that you know very well doesn't serve you any more, live the life that you choose knowing is what makes you happy. Love is always or sometimes difficult to find where is trustworthy and you can hate everything that you are when all of this begins to happen to you. Except that you can have so much as well, and the most complicated situation becoming easy to thrive through. Is what we fail to see at some point in our lives as we're not paying attention to what we need to be.

The more we pay attention to what we passionate about, a new level reveals itself, and at times you don't need to wander around, all that we love does come to us. When we have done our part, and that includes our deepest desires. If you still feel like you have to figure what truly inspires you, then you're not where you need to be. Find yourself and be content of who you are, then strive for it to reach that success level which satisfies you.

If you ever get to that place where you have achieved that kind of understanding through your knowledge, you have arrived where your ambitions makes sense. Is always sad how situations will make you feel, knowing very well we cannot be wrong about ourselves. Not when you have discovered a true purpose, you just let go of everything and allow fate to drive you.

Normally we all feel everything that we entitled to, and you know how to value if something is worth the price, then you can be able to tell that here I have received a bargain. Is not like we don't see, or realize the importance, so much we could've had anyhow, only that with growth a lot changed and moved into a level where we have to deserve. We must be worthy of who we are, and to have worked hard to be in a position to receive exactly what we are.

So ironic how things have changed from what we use to know to something else, and when you hadn't worked hard you saw the results of that. Where even what you know is rightfully yours became taken away, so strive to resemble that kind of understanding, and knowledge with faith. While you holding on to this new identity that you have where you know what you worth, as difficult as it could be, hoping for the best out of life.

You have buried your past and now you are about the future, you want tomorrow to be very fruitful as well, and that's the part you have been struggling with. To have your goals realized and everything that you deserve coming through the path you have chosen for yourself, which has turn out not easy to understand and be what you can rely on.

So much can hold you back, and not to forget that you as well are there to delay your progress, when you lack confidence in your desired objective. You want your worth to reveal itself, and see the person that you have chosen come alive, though a lot is meant to tie us down. However you as well must choose what is important to you, so that you can act upon it, and nobody can ever stand in your way.

The battlefield is very small, is within you and choosing what you desire, so you see the part where the world is not the enemy. So much out here is a reflection of our faith and what we are or what we seek to be, even love could be like that. Is more like marrying the person that you are, is who you are on the inside revealed on the outside.

As you see the results of who you are, ask yourself, is this what you love about you? Everything we experience is our faith revealed to witness what we are deep within. So how do you want to make your life, or become a human being, and plans, is called having planned all that you wanted to be rightly and on time? You can or can't make peace with what you are, but is the outcome of the path you have chosen and it can change.

If you can choose to see something different, a new world has just begun, and it doesn't have to take forever to become a reality. You can think everything that you desire to be right now and see it come to life, there's not much standing in our way, we are what stands in our path to success. Therefore can you give up on that old way you've been holding on to, so that you can become a new person.

Can you stay the same, or rather put everything behind, and reach for your deepest desires, even if it means that for now or for a very long time you just keep on struggling with it? Is when your heart had been set on something that you not sure where you headed and how you will arrive there, a dream that no longer serves a purpose.

If is really what you love, why not dedicate all your attention to it, even if it means that it consumes every last energy you have. As failure to understand has so much to question about how prepared are you? So you learn to value who you are and what you need, even when the way seems to be a little hard to understand, you adapt to it.

Unless you don't have it within you, so you think about it carefully, not only once, every day if pursuing this life isn't an excuse you have to neglect your responsibilities, and if you not you will know as you will be motivated to go on.

Regardless of how we lie to ourselves, some things are clear to see, and we can be able to tell where we are. You know your progress, you might not be aware how far you still need to travel. Now that you wouldn't choose to be something you couldn't be for yourself, you not scared, as you know how furthermore you required to proceed and how you will get there.

Although the way is filled with so much questioning who we are and how prepared we are to go all out. Since it isn't something that you study somewhere, and you're needed to resemble true understanding. As it is your own ideas seeking to bring you out of the invisible into life. So you cannot overlook that period where you have to perfect everything and be creative.

As it doesn't matter how it came about, you need to reach that level of excellence, you take away the fantasy and create reality like it hasn't been seen. You circle that lack of confidence in human knowledge, and make something good happens. You pass so many levels of expectations and surprise the world with the beauty of art and creativity.

So live to convince yourself of the life you desire to see, as it will not happen until you make it possible. Regardless of how likely we are to find ourselves alone, and so vulnerable to relationships, and you can try to adopt feeling the need to hold on to love you're not even sure exists inside.

Hoping that it will be better, and it won't, the burden just becomes too much and you tying down your own progress. Whatever you are only means that much to you, and there are not many who understand what you are, as the path by which everyone travels is easy and free.

You are estranged in your dreams in a life that only make sense to you, we not saying don't reach for the stars, go for it. See yourself being born the way you like in this world of understanding, and through your unique ideas. Even so, don't be a stranger, or left out of everything that love has to offer, you are someone with needs as well, so make your part count, be recognizable, and held back a little.

Only that you mustn't be late to find true meaning to all that exists, you might never get used to being part of everything good. Arrive where you matter, and come back from where you have died, you cannot be that invalid to see the way back to being human. So serve that idea for so much must come to pass, although our hearts and soul keeps holding on to the past, it will eventually disappear as a new chapter begins.

How do we justify all these efforts that we give to a life of creativity, if we're not prepared to be successful and live through it? So much can be ruined from the time you've dedicated and you could be left behind forever. If you ever want to have something good, adapt to what you have become. That can lead you back to being human instead of living isolated from everything that matters.

Everything can come at whatever point in your life, what you ought to have done is to be prepared more than you were yesterday. You need to give that extra energy for all your heart desires to come to be, some things are not held back by the goal you have inside.

It is within your reach and you can achieve it by sacrificing some part of who you are, and it exists on the same level. It just wants you to move out of your comfort zone and be on a path you're prepared to travel to have whatever you desire out of this creative atmosphere.

You can almost feel lost with no idea on how to tackle your situations. Only if you can just be faithful to all that you are and what you require, realize the goal when it is what has become the priority, and when that opportunity comes, seize it. Knowing that you can never be that person, or wonder about the same thing again.

Is everything that you are and what you desire out of life, and nothing comes free. You must be willing to pay the price for what you truly love. Do not be scared, understand why you need to make something out of it, you cannot keep resenting yourself forever.

When we keep missing the opportunities that are always given to us, ask yourself who is not doing their part? You could be the one that is failing to make things happen. You can abandon what you have for something new to come to life. Still, you must know what's at stake as the situation is no longer normal, and you need to have a sharp eye.

As you can continue abandoning things until you're left with nothing to live for. On the contrary, do you know when is time to start accumulating everything you require back to you, is what you must understand, to let go and to take back.

There's a world you rejected to become what you passionate about, then there must be something you fall in love with so bad you would do anything to be part of. It could be a good relationship that you long for, as lonely as life can get, you must set your heart on it as it could be waiting for you on the other side. Free and true to have, if you willing to commit to it. You need to understand how to make it work, as we are not completely consumed all over our lives, some things are there to give us back what we have lost. You just need to open your eyes given that it could be time to start earning something worthy of you.

So many have never known the exact cause of their solitude, although when you have seen where things have gone wrong, how can you not come back from such a setback? At times you need to sacrifice all that you are right now to be human again, even if so much could be against the person that you are. Only that you don't have to let so much passes you, instead of sitting there and feeling sorry for yourself, accusing people of not understanding who you are.

You can take that leap of faith into what you love the most, even if is not you who keeps resenting the other, and yes so much can steal that tenderness of life. Still, when something has presented itself as an opportunity to become all that you seek out of life, then jump on it, and hold on tight to avoid remaining behind forever.

We are never as left back as we think we are, it could be whatever that has led to this situation. You can find your way back, unfulfilled goals can lead to one living an incomplete life. Now from just any effort in the right direction you can wake up from that deep sleep, you just need to be faithful to something. So if you are true to your work, you will get that out of everything, and be precise of what you seek out of all that exists out there.

As so much will present itself to you, only if you have a perfect picture of what you truly desire, then you can never go wrong, in knowing how to make use of it. As the way is full of surprises, some will be there to give you what you want, while others are there to take away everything you have. So remember that you have to be strong for what you need, as you are not abandoned, your life is there as well, and will be yours when you deserve.

Chapter Six

Remember to Love

You work hard every day until you get used to it, so much that you forget about what is the most important thing in life, love, how to care, and look after your loved ones. Especially if you began this path without anyone to keep closer to your heart. These spiritual activities we engage in becomes the only thing that matters before everything we have as responsibilities towards the lives we living. How do we let something that we not even certain we will succeed in doing, steal away that tenderness we have for all that we are?

You let that be the only objective you have to fulfill before you can be able to commit to anything, so much you only have a space for that in your heart. Love was always a stranger, or rather strange, wherever it came from. You always look forward to being loved for what you do as you feel that's necessary, and when you not getting things right. You preserve yourself hoping that if you ever figure things out, someone who truly deserves what you are, will come and fill that emptiness in your life.

We are never sure why the need to commit to so much that we do, however love of all things, how can you live without it? You could have wished to justify the end as the only place where a lot will make sense, still, that kind of loneliness takes everything, and the memories you have ever valued. That longing for someone you have loved every day or wished to continue to care for your whole life.

Makes you linger there, and there's just no making peace with it, and it becomes unbearable when you don't know when you will reach that point of success. Now you have to put that behind, and focus on something which has become pain through the dedication you suppose to give.

As every day passes and there's no one to hold, or care for you, a week becomes a lifetime. How you wished to be touched where you tenderly, and now for a longer period there won't be any. You feel miserable, when you know is not going to happen any time soon, and part of that you can never know if is a good or a bad thing. Given that you are only left with yourself to count on, rotating with your responsibilities through the days. Hoping to get things right, so that true love can come and be truthful or rescue you.

As we have that need and it can never disappear regardless of how dedicated we are to doing things. It keeps on seeking for us to give in more to love, and as our hearts become formed by reality and the truth. We begin to realize what we truly desire, and instead of getting stronger you become weaker by the day, and you wonder if the loneliness will ever go away.

Does being alone gives us the space we need to choose precisely what we really want? As an individual who has given themselves to achieving a certain goal. You only wish for the world of true love to have revealed itself before all these journeys began, and why is it the only thing that takes away the joy we deserve to be happy?

Who truly needs our true love, so much that we cannot hold it back for some time and focus on something else? As so much questions if is really important to walk away from love in that way. Maybe is when you have failed doing things right that you can decide to isolate yourself and find that unique quality in you, that will make you feel content once more. Even when you will suffer the strain of what you desire to be human again, and you cannot say it will be better soon when you don't know what tomorrow will bring.

Do you even remember how to be there for someone who cares about you, or loves you that much? And worse is that you as well are not coping with the person you have become. You feeling lost and abandoned, as if no one cares, and everybody was there, you walked out of the love you had by seeking recognition or a proper life.

Now you want to know where you can find it again as original as it was from the beginning, untainted with, very strong and bold that is everything to live for. We walk away from so much just to find that true quality in being an individual, it becomes something that you need to be confident in with finding true love.

As much as you have lost touch with all of life, is part of you that keeps pushing those you have around you to find itself. Now at the end, can you accept being loved again, or cared for? To have walked away opens a gap that cannot be closed overnight. What are we actually walking apart from, and what do we seek to find, is there any reason other than wanting more out of life? Is there no other way that we can have all that we need and still be content of love, as you couldn't continue with what you were?

We walk away from the love we have, hoping to find some quality in being an individual, a star, someone that is who you are on an intellectual level. You saw it unfit to continue and build the legacy you dream of on top of what you currently are, and you seek a new foundation. One which you don't have right now, and if you want something that will change all that you've ever known, then you need to begin somewhere.

As what you are isn't enough to proceed with, when you refuse to establish yourself, above what you were, you obviously are not satisfied with what you have been. You require a fresh start, which could be influenced by modernization, being good or anything.

We might be required to look thoroughly to understand if we are on the right path, and how do you know that with whatever you striving for you will reach what you hoping for? And enough for people to love you and that someone worthy will come along, and give you that everlasting joy you deserve to live happily ever after. As you had known that to commit is important, but you had to put something else before it. So that you can derive happiness from its success, and everything will not matter until then.

That's the thing with people who have find a purpose to go beyond the ordinary substances to discover a life that so many haven't understood. We have changed our focus from loving a human being, and plant a seed of love for this world, a person no longer comes first. Our minds are not obsessed with getting ahead in relationships, we have started devoting our attention to discovering our universe. No more objectives of when to do something that resembles caring, now we are only concern with achieving goals.

Goals have become the building block for our entire well-being, we forget how beautiful it is to be always giving all that we are to the people who care about us, and they need that much commitment. In a way that after they have left our lives is not them who suffer the consequences of the relationship we had, is who we are. Deep within we become so hollow that we don't even know what to live for any more, and you never understand what is the best solution to what you have become, to move on with life or to go back.

Above all is always important that you reach a solution to whatever you seek to invent yourself soon enough to be content. As it is better to have left so much behind and succeed on your new route, than to be found lost along the way that you constantly look behind hoping for something to make sense, and it never does.

Whereas what you require is to give in completely to a way forward, when the need to understand is there, and deep down inside you have a lot of love. You must allow that feeling to show how much you care, not only for that special person. For family, as well as those around you, by a way of reaching that place you want to be.

As much as you long to be together with those you value the most, still, it will be better on the other side when you have triumphant, and when you not certain of where you going, and what you really want. You keep remaining behind spiritually and hurting so many who care about you, is when you haven't decided what could be the best thing to do.

You refuse to completely give in, your mind continuously goes back and that suffocates a lot of who need you intact. When you hold love closer to your heart, other than just to live whatever you find as life. Comes a time where you must give all that you are, and never remember what you use to be.

You start by building faith in your capabilities, even though we require that much from those with expertise to help us reach our full potential. It is the needs we have that makes us feel incapable of being the solution to our problems, and whatever we seek keeps taking more of who we are, until we're left feeling worthless. Your whole faith based in your knowledge, soon becomes the better option.

You begin to see the bigger side of you, and it doesn't matter who you rely on, only that you don't need the dependency in human beings. It explains that you are behind in whatever you want out of life. The future based in your own will cannot hurt you like you will affect those who loves you, when you not working on perfecting yourself.

The sooner you invest in your knowledge you learn to become more to what you want, and it can be beautiful. Regardless of what you require from those you have built dependency on, and is not that they cannot help you or give you what you want. Is to love what you have turn out to be, so much feels better when you know what you doing, and dedicating your whole life to discover a lot about yourself. The star coming alive in you is learning to stand in your own will, what we are can be everything that we want out of this world, if we let it be.

Remembering how to love, care, or be there when someone needs you, is very meaningful regardless of what you doing. That is resembling how concerned you are for their well-being, and not to want someone when you are in need, that isn't kind or caring either. You are required to give the best of your life to those you keep closer at whatever point, it doesn't have to be about needing anything from each other. It could be the support that matters, always realize the flow that goes on between human beings, and strive to keep the balance.

Love is the balance of human nature, though isn't what we usually strive for before we reach our goals. We feel good settling for it when we have reached our full potential, and it is great as you're able to have a mutual input in it. As you mustn't forget that everyone is hoping to gain something from that union which has brought you together.

If someone cares about you and you don't return the favor, it hurts to the other. Stop and ask yourself what are we benefiting from being with each other? As one must feel lucky to have you in their lives that is how a relationship should be like, a two way flow that gives and take.

Who have you remembered how to love lately, care for, nurture, or anything that is showing affection? As we never know where it begins and where it ends. Who often needs you to be there for them, and why do you need them back? Your family, friends, and that special person who not only loves you, also gave themselves to you more than anyone.

Which one forms part of our responsibility and which doesn't? You can obsess with getting ahead, and never making enough time to please someone. Only that after a very long time is you who will suffer the setback from not making quality time to find joy.

So much can have a lot of people hurting as this kind of responsibilities are part of what we take willingly, and is not something common about human beings. That being the reason why they might feel very unwelcome at some point, only if you learn to focus on the love you have in your heart. You change so much and improve your well-being and relationship with others, you might not be late in every angle of life. You could be early somewhere, where you are truly valued, and that is what could make sense about living happy.

This paths we take towards our own understanding is what motivates life for one to be exciting. At the end of the day, you find yourself committing to it so much you have no time to socialize with friends and family. Now as much as you love working in your own way of thinking, that has in turn created a distance from all the people you were supposed to be there for.

It always starts as a minor thing which might seem to have no direction, as you go on it begins to take over everything that you are. Before you arrive where you wanted to, you are found wondering about what you intended to be.

Can you ever find yourself where you matter, where you are not only focused on your well-being? Somebody who understands others and has created a room for them as well, and has made time to be there for those who need you that much. Will love ever come to exist in you, true love filled with caring which isn't consuming for those around you?

Just giving, sharing, and kind enough to actually be there when someone requires of you. That holds on to everyone who wants you in their lives, and understand why you must be there, and how to make the most of each and every moment.

It must at times be a mutual feeling when is meant to be, as it wouldn't be true love if it isn't something we both feel the same about. Our fair share of happiness, and beside the fact that is where we actually matter to each other, is the gift we have inherited from life itself.

The good part about everything that we are, when you're not within that cycle of love, you could be stuck and suffocating. You might not know now, and is what it is, it will catch up with you, and sooner or later you will need all those people who share that sense of connectivity with you.

It isn't likely that you can walk away from what you have right now, and come across people who will circle your life with kindness. You might find one who is willing to go the extra mile, still, that would be the only person who was able to adjust their lives to make a room for you and all your needs.

It usually doesn't come easy, it takes so much, to find that kind of caring, it happens most of the time that things would have remained the same. So since you went out in search for more of who you are, so much started building on top of one another. Before you know it, there is no space for someone, and things begins to fall apart.

As people we have deep connections, our relationships are determined by so much. In some situations we are usually related by blood, and that is what forms the bonds we cannot easily break between us, as human beings, and is what pulls us to need each other. We require part of one another every day to complement our daily progress or success.

When someone is stuck, you who is a close relative to that person are able to pull that particular individual out of their situation. The relationship continues like that forever, into something we cannot explain about us needing part of the other.

So imagine leaving that behind and heading to the outside world, where there's hardly anyone that you know. Where everything is a complete stranger to all that you are, or desire out of life, and to what forms part of the person you are on the inside. Though you cannot cut that connection you had with family. Now you seek a new beginning, one which is your own, and you never know what isn't enough for someone to walk away from what they had, to start something which is meant for them to be happy.

Now you let go of all that you are to find something that you worth deep down inside. True love in the next life is your new beginning, the foundation to everything that you want to be through your own vision. You allow someone to come closer to you, to form part of your future, and that is how you open up your heart to commit to that special person, who finds it in them to trust you with their well-being. You share that mutual understanding and begin to surrender yourself to each other's lives, until you create that bond with one another.

Bonds are the strongest we can ever achieve in a relationship as they can never be broken, they form an eternal union of hearts that can never be separated. Which is what we always had from the beginning, and walked away from, in search of something real. In our next chapter kids form an everlasting connection we have with each other, they are the new foundation we have with life.

Knowing that you gave yourself for that to happen from true love, which wasn't easy to arrive at. Still, you were able to find that within you, and therefore making sure it was genuine love that has founded all that you truly desire.

You could be someone continuing in the same heritage of love and life which you're not happy about, and the deeper you connect the more you destroy the human being that you are. The thing is that if you have realized an opportunity to become something else, it could be that you are not pleased with what you are, and if that pushes you to feel a need for change. Then it is personal and only about you and what you understand about yourself, and that's the thing about people you never really know the nature of a person.

Is only within them where they get to understand the kind of feeling they have towards life. It becomes more of an individual path, no two people can respond the same to how they feel about things. If you're completely satisfied with how you were born, then you have that way as your own, and you can continue with it.

As you can never share that kind of understanding with anyone, and we have that option from birth. To make sense of what we need and desire out of this world, and create our own point of view about how we see things, which is something that will make you happy.

The question that you need to ask yourself is that, is it really worth it to walk away from all that you have, to start a new foundation somewhere? Since you obviously walked out from a companionship which you had with everyone that you loved as you were not satisfied about it.

You allowed the union to divide in between and become a new person which you know wasn't easy, still invited it in your world. What is it that you were not happy with which could be that bad, that you can no longer take being a similar person made by the same bonds out of life?

What is it that is worthy of the sacrifice you making, as so much can touch us deep within where we fragile, and now you're a different person, and is just not who you are any more. It has got to that point where it must create in your life, and you know that I'm being made wrong, for all that I am, I'm being turned by situations. Given that when it gets to that level where it forces you to become something else then there's a real need for change. Be someone that is your heart's deepest desire, and not to be a stranger to yourself.

Could a change be necessary regardless of how you were born and raised, or maybe you saw how you were made into this world, and understood that this isn't the kind of life you want to rejoice about. You felt a need to start your own family which will have a base of real love. As that's what we lack in most instances, that foundation of true love which will give us anything we require, and we grow up with it. Just that we can never be forced to have that as our only way to being human forever, you have your option to become something that you truly desire.

No one is ever forced to become something they're not happy about, we never have our lives decided for us before we are born into this life. We decide very well that we will be something that is our own invention, and our will, you don't allow anything to make that decision for you. Even as part of the journey you have to take on your own, you don't let situations make that choice for you. The quest to understanding, to be that unique individual, is to rise up against anything which could stand to oppose the person that you are.

Things usually have a very innocent beginning, and you can settle for it when you don't really require all that is good and quality from life. When you begin to seek for something more, which is who you are deep within, you start to suffer from the way you were born and raised. Those bonds from your foundation are still binding you with the same way you were meant to follow, and then you find it unworthy and decide to take your own turn. As so much can stand in your way, so bad that you can fight countless battles to come back to the person that you have chosen to be.

Still you can never have that solution easily, and the best thing is to have humble beginnings which will pave a way for the kind of person that you will be. At the end of the day we choose who we are, and what we want to be, there has to be a way to stop something which you not happy about. It could have been a generation curse that followed your family for years, at some point one has to end it.

Like it is said we all have that little demon that we must fight out of our lives to have a brand new life that we could be able to rejoice about, and it does matter when it happens. As much as you mustn't care how long you have been suffocating from it.

The only essential thing that should be the matter right now is that you were able to start afresh. Your life will never be the same, and is very amazing as we can never have the same solution to the problems we facing. We can have it whichever way suits our needs, and maybe that's the reason it is so difficult to breakout of situations, in a way that is common about us human beings. As we usually go through different spiritual battles which we need to break away from, and you don't know what something could be pulling you to become.

Only that you can have your own solution, it doesn't have to suffocate you every day, is when you know that here I have an option and I can become what I want for myself. I don't have to be driven to a place I don't feel the need to belong. It could be that at the end you have nothing to live for except to be that person that you know you are, and that individual lives deep in your soul, where the magic of life is. You loved all that you are, and valued it where it matters, as whether we feel a reason to accept it is about value.

Not everybody is supposed to hate the way they were born in order to have a new beginning. You can have a good base which is to die for, and your life has been blessed from that. So you continue with it, embracing it, celebrating how you were made into this world, as that's what we become, after all has changed. You are now left with this new platform which will be the foundation of good only, and that doesn't take away your will to be a human being that you require, be whatever you need to be.

You just begin right where you are and take it further, continue in the heritage that has been passed down to you. Since what we really need is a good foundation which maybe could be hard to find, only that if we ever reach for it. We hold on to it with everything that we have, and we give so much that we are to make the most of that life. As the thief is always after every precious possession that we have, so we fight for it. In order to keep it for the rest of our lives, knowing that if you don't have a way to make use of it, you can lose it all.

Chapter Seven

Reaching Out for Love

It is so much that we need out of life that remains hidden from us human beings. Things like money, and everything that we desire which forms part of the materialistic possession, as for love it has always been here. Is just that careers are very important and we are required to do something about that part of who we are, as early as possible, and you must choose your career carefully. So that you can have whatever you want, happiness comes from being satisfied with that side of our lives.

If you are not happy with your profession, you might resent to so much. We put a lot on hold just to have that one part of our lives realized, and you can feel satisfied with what you are currently. While you can lose it all as well, as your life is meaningless without a very strong background that speaks for you. A career is a statement that you make without having to say so much about yourself, and when you keep that up. You have everything that you desire from that point which becomes the measure of success.

It measures how far you supposed to have things, what you entitled to, do you deserve that most beautiful relationship you fantasizing about? Are you worth that luxurious car and a house that you dreaming about? All of it makes up for who you are, and that's why we give up everything that we have for that to become ours. As we can spend days and years lost in love thinking that something went wrong. While so much broke down there, when you couldn't keep up with things, you lost your entire life.

We are not only required to get what we want, at times we are also tested on whether we do deserve what we worth. Are we the kind of people that must hold on to who they are, and what they have? Or we can be discriminated as we don't possess enough knowledge, its life, it goes around that, and we don't grow up like that? We are only trapped into that kind of situation when your time to be responsible comes, after you could've lost touch with so much as you needed time to rethink your strategies.

Now is a period to have it all back, and so many settle for less when they reach at these stages, they refuse to see through the struggle of growth in love. They allow themselves to be compromised by the obstacles they encounter, and therefore take the easy way out, and it doesn't always have to be like that.

You can come back after the world has tested your patience and capabilities to have it all again. You can have love where is quality, and when you find that nature of acceptance in someone, who can take it away from you? For some reason we deny ourselves what is rightfully ours, and we can awaken once more, and see what we need to break through the struggle, the devotion we are required to possess. We don't just break out of our current lives to have something good especially what you've always dreamed of, you must do everything necessary for which part of life is dependent on.

It says so much about an individual, along the way it becomes our new identity, the only thing that you need to become what you truly desire. When you don't focus on something important, you fail to see the part where you must develop yourself in terms of finding quality life, and you can overlook that. Only later to pay the price for all that you've neglected, and you can give up on the love you know very well you deserve, since you fail to put up with the battle that is required of you. Unlike giving up, resemble a very strong character that is worthy of whatever you passionate about.

So if you didn't realize that part of yourself is fine, you can struggle for some time with it to come back to reality again, don't lose hope too early, when is true love that you looking for. Do not compromise that gift for something that we are, if it means that for a long time you remain isolated for it to become true once more, then do it. Along the way it becomes the only thing to live for outside everything that we know.

We actually don't get to see this part of our life at the beginning of our journey to adulthood, and is there to last forever. You have to be very quick in understanding everything that you desire to be, you cannot remain stuck forever. Set free your passion, and be able to arrive where all your heart's desires are answered, no heartache, and everything you want is now achievable, and content of who you are.

By failing to understand what you need at the beginning, you're remaining without true love for a long run. We have responsibilities standing before our happiness, as something that we cannot see that it will affect our whole lives. Again it reflects so much about an individual to realize how important that part of our life is, and not to look away. It doesn't feel like it is necessary at the foundation, it only becomes what is true about us at the end.

The only thing we have to live for if you ever want to find happiness. It is able to build a connection with your deepest desires, and then you're able to make sense of everything within that context of life, success, and relationships. When you are done with your career path, what remains a mystery is love, it becomes what we struggle for to be true.

To have someone giving themselves to us permanently, however you as well on the other hand must be standing on the side that is very welcoming. If you don't make it safe for that special person to feel free to occupy your heart, it might be difficult for one to let go of who they are into your arms.

If you fail to do your part you can wake up with nothing to show for, is not a matter of whether you had something or not. Your own career on the other hand through your understanding derives quality from life. You can inherit so much and become content of yourself, for some reason it will show, with love is like you're also reflected on it. When you haven't done your part it becomes something that can be felt easily, and when you have played your role that can be seen too.

At the end is not like you wasting time by building a profession that will stand out, as you will witness a lot becoming life from that point of understanding. You can be hard on yourself on whether you could've been a failure to be working on things which only make sense to you, and if you don't know why.

It could be that we become formed in the path of our desires, and that is the only reality we get from doing what we good at, and we do it spontaneously without knowing why. Maybe is quality of the heart, when you need to have the best out of everything that becomes the only way, easy to have done things.

There's a need for that kind of commitment as it is life, there's nothing above it, is the only way to happiness. We don't know why, somehow it feels right, and if you not doing it for love then it is not worth it. The value and the price is when you know that something beautiful out there exists, and you preparing yourself for all of it.

Whether it takes one day or many to become success or possible, is how you must go for it, reach for it and see how deserving you are. When your heart is still vacant, give commitment to what you want out of been an individual. It will become the concrete platform by which you stand on to find true love for someone.

Two brought together by love are hard to find, and we are meant to live like that to be happy. Only that we don't know what keeps the union alive, yet the other one who is important in making that a reality is who you are, and you must be devoted to it. Well developed and prepared so that you can make that quality of life happens, and not to give yourself where you're important too easy. As you have failed to see the way, and we lose so much from that.

When you have compromised your objectives since you not fulfilling your way to fullness, you can linger out there, unstable about what you really need. Only when you have arrived where your personal goals are clear that so much become settled, and you will not be shaken in any area of your well-being. As everything fears someone with well-defined character.

A lot pushes us to test if we still value that worthiness we suppose to possess, if we are to have the best out of life. Do you even have that eager to do things for so much, where have you given up or compromised that sense of satisfaction? As it happens along the way when you have worked to fulfill your objectives, that you become so strongly focused.

You begin to have the perfect description of the person you want to spend the rest of your life with, and you can hold on to so many lies, thinking that you don't know the importance of working hard. While deep in your heart you understand that is the worth of what awaits ahead that matters.

You have seen love, and how beautiful it is to be involved with someone who matters. The value of all the days you spend together, and we continuously refuse to admit it to ourselves that we have a natural thing which guides us towards what we truly deserve. Otherwise you wouldn't have known how to travel this far, and you can criticize yourself, when you continue to work for what you believe in. Thinking it doesn't serve a purpose, whereas it does, and what is not worthy of your objectives on the other hand is letting go of what could've earned you a chance to have your innermost desire.

While you work for whatever you believe in, you create the perfect picture of the love you have inside. Is like art, only that this time you sculpting your love life, and is love where is quality. Unlike what we settle for along the way, as we are scared to confront the world about everything that we desire.

You can ask yourself countless questions, like what have I done to deserve this kind of luck. While you worked for it, and is good, to understand the value of what we are or do and what opportunities it opens for us. You could have grown up as a meek person that you could've shy away from so much.

Then you acknowledge that you have aged, and there's no need to be reserved any more as everything becomes a necessity, or maybe we can say that you never saw the use of something until it was essential. Now how do you deal with that, and as we are born worthy, the odds could still be in your favor and they allow you to have what you worth easily, and without having to try so hard.

Unfortunately for those who have ruined their lives at a early age they need a second chance, and when things don't go right. You wonder what could have gone wrong, and is who you are, you have brought that to life through your way of doing things. As we are continuously questioned for our worthiness, or maybe if you still feel deserving.

You can work hard to create a platform where you will be worthy of all that you want, and that will allow you to have everything. True love is created from that through our understanding as well, what you are or understand becomes the love that the world has blessed you with.

What if you never knew so much about life? Then do right and remain worthy. Let those who are involved in the sophistication of the world discover their true potential and what beauty awaits them ahead, as they have known that much, and they deserve it. Is the experience that we have that determines the kind of path we travel, for some it could have been different, love was always there, and remained like that forever. Unlike those who grew up bound by priorities, and didn't see any difference, and only became aware of the need to be loving someone, when it was a necessity.

For those who grew up in love, living through it, in and out of time, they could've experience the difference, and witness the change in behaviour. They saw what they didn't have and where it had failed them, and became human beings who need to work hard for them to acquire so that they can deserve. So much can at times be difficult for someone who has to labor to be normal.

Along the way you could've become weak as you couldn't afford to be part of the life you required, and that is the period that has led so many to have been alone when they needed to understand themselves. Situations required you isolated to think thoroughly of what you doing, and how to reach all that you desire.

So when you begin to feel the need to prepare yourself for the rest of your life, you not only preparing to be content of your own world. You reaching out there, to all the hearts that are vacant and available for love. You communicating with human beings similar to what you are, you writing your name in someone's heart, so they can save a space for you.

Asking for that special person to clear their heart so to come and occupy it, and you can choose how far you want to make your part heard. We design our lives from zero to the end, is what you are willing to give in, that you will have back.

You can never really appreciate being loved until you see the part where it is so magnificent. The fact that you paint your love, it is unbelievable how you can design your relationship. Without understanding how that came to happen, that tender of all that we are forms the most important quality of our values.

Without it where is true we have been robbed of so much, and only remaining with so little to live for, and you can never tell the difference. Whether is real or not until you find someone who was created by your perception, how that particular individual complements who you are far deep.

Whether is all in our hands or maybe is just love, and the way things are, there's no luck there. Is not like accidentally picking a coin from the ground, is choosing your partner from among so many who are people. In a world where human beings are normal they think so much through before giving themselves to someone, and you must allow that quality of your life to come alive. Be enough for that special person to give themselves to you without hesitations.

We are never intelligent enough to be sure of everything we need to have become to live life freely. We allow so much to happen at its natural state without care of what it could have been under different circumstances. Even if we want to live effortlessly, there's love in this world that came to you through your efforts, it was not by an accident. You have to seek for it, and as we strive to reach our full potential, so much become possible, and is the results of what we yearning for, you brought it to reality.

When you are not sure of who you are, you can hate yourself, and how would you wish for the best when you despise everything that you are. You can feel like taking the easy way out, if you don't know what's at stake. So if you knew that is not just a minor thing you giving up on, you wouldn't want to stop or quit. Would you walk away from that part of your understanding knowing is capable of blessing you with all that you need?

You can be deeply lost in love, how would you say is the perfect way for deserving man and woman, to just meet and it feels so right. As is the way it must be, something has brought us together, and that thing is so strong inside and about who we are. Could being destined for a certain thing have anything to do with it?

If you were to bring out an argument, between destiny and love, what would you say is the best answer? What controls what we are, does fate control our lives, and is there anything inside ourselves of that nature? Or is the path that I have begun which I have traveled so far from the beginning which becomes my determination for true love, which takes over everything that we are.

What channels our energy in the right direction, and gives us strength especially in situations where you would've given up, or maybe you know you didn't do right and you have failed? But came back to become exactly what you needed to be at the end, how do you justify your life towards that part of success which the way became like a maze? Yet you ended up reaching your goals and heart desires. The wonder to that is how you got the best out of everything, and you are fully aware that traveling that journey through your understanding didn't make any sense.

You got lost at some point, so much didn't make sense, you failed in so many ways and passed one which became your life. How were you able to identify yourself and find your inner passion, or just to understand what you needed to be? And when it wasn't you traveled a different path that never led you where you wanted to arrive at.

How did you discover what you love about you deeply? Maybe is the child in us that get lost, and when you're prepared to mature something which is fate is there to pull us back to reality. Arouses the interest in us to focus in a certain direction which you must travel through.

How would you justify losing so much time, and coming back to matter again? Is there anything that deep inside we need to take care of, which is ourselves that knows what we deserve? Even if it would've been difficult, is something that believes in our capabilities to achieve the best. Which is more devoted to our well-being, better than we are, and is the ultimate driver.

Although we refuse to accept it, somehow is what created our lives where you acknowledges that this is what I wouldn't have done for myself, and whatever you wanted has happened. It became life for everyone to see, that thing is what you failed to ruin about you, when for a very long time you couldn't do things right, it had remained focused.

When you were not ready and you couldn't do anything to help yourself, it was stronger than you. Even where you lacked knowledge of what you were doing, when you hadn't mastered anything. It became the only thing that knew how to work for your welfare, and maybe is that thing that we have to pass in us which indicates that we now understand what we stand for.

Is something which for a defined period of time could still be opposing us if we have failed to see. It represents our point of views as human beings who haven't find who we are, and when you have passed your understanding, it disappears. It was there to care for you, your needs, and protect you, maybe is will power.

So if there is something that looks after all that we are, which cannot trust us with ourselves, and until you know what you doing, you're not free. Can that thing which is who we are when we don't understand what we doing be trustworthy enough, to care for relationships in our lives?

Can you trust anything with the true love you're required to have as a person, or that is just settling for anything, and love becomes quality when you have taken over your own life? When that happens and you are fully knowledgeable, then you can take control of everything that you desire. Could we just need to be deserving, and that is enough to win a good heart?

So what would you settle for? Love that is quality, which is created by your understanding, as regardless of what you don't understand or seem to know about life. Not knowing or being unaware of who you are seems to take a little out of what would have been complete happiness, and then you have to accept that. As if opening a door to acceptance has opened a gate for so much that needs to be accepted, by not being aware of what is happening, things seems to hide away.

They want to turn themselves into natural situations, whereas they're not, love is hiding from us there, and so much isn't how it must be. Something is missing as we're not content, there's a crime for what we've lost, if you go after your passion a lot seems to respect you for that. It doesn't seem like as much as we require is free or affordable, and you must pay the price, if you don't the thief of life and true love comes after everything you have. You wake up and you don't have enough of what you want, what happened to the person that you were.

So much does not justify who we are and what we want to be, it became necessary when you needed true quality out of life. You don't have to learn or understand after you've lost everything that you are to this world. So imagine if you've never worked for anything that you became compromised. The work has never been seen fit before we reach this level where we are, or until you need love, and you don't have to come back after something has gone wrong trying to rectify the only thing you could've done right at the beginning.

So true love seems to be the only thing we need that we ought to have worked hard for. Which isn't always easy to get, and it breaks one's heart to think about it or finding it, whereas you can never have it that simple. You can struggle all the way with who you are and what you have become, still, you can't, is hard to find someone who is true to love, and you can convince yourself thinking you have found the one.

Only that when you haven't done your part to the end, you haven't met the one. Reaching for that special person means becoming content of you first, when you are now sure of who you are and what you truly want out of life. Then you can have a real relationship, is what you are and what you know that pulls the same thing out of this world back to you.

Finding true love has never been the easiest thing to understand, but there are so many relationships. Of which we don't know the nature of their commitments and communions, or what eats them on the inside. What fight so much for human beings not to have happiness, as some just stay in it since they have to, and it becomes love for so many who don't care. Knowing it isn't there, or how is supposed to be, a complete devotion has a way of creating real warmth and for a very long time you can never be lost. You become filled with joy for discovering such a gift of something so true about ourselves.

The fact that you can never know the story between two people makes it hard enough to assume there could be happiness. Many families are based on that philosophy of love, to hang in there, to hold on to what they have. However there's true love in this life that is just how everything must be, it is so pure, so blessed and happy. That you can never ask for anything more, relationships like that are there, and makes so much difference. Can you believe it, how rare that kind of commitment is to find? And it all lies within you, and what you need.

Do you understand the nature of this communion? Although at the end love is there that is common at a equilibrium level of everything that we are, and rather not too hard to find. While is something to live for, and for those many souls who can never break out of the system and understand themselves. That will be the quality of life and true love, which is where the majority have found themselves living happily ever after, at a platform where all that we are is balanced.

So if you never knew how to be balanced what would you settle for? As everything is too low for someone to call a life, and that is just the part of everything you didn't know about this world. You as well could've never guessed that the path which you have taken is never enough, you only get to see when you begin to seek and you can't find. That you need something genuine to call true love, and that's when you begin to work for your good, and if you breakthrough your understanding, you will be happy ever after.

Chapter Eight

Allies of the Angel Life

Where do you find someone that cares about you, or what you doing, who has been officially made for you, though you feel like you are never focused on love. Maybe your time has been wasted by work night and day, and you're deeply lost that you don't know where to get that unique individual.

Who can give you everything that you deserve, and what you will discover is hard to believe, that there's always an open heart ready to receive you, and your innermost desire. You just have to understand how to travel to that place where all that you are fits in. Everyone has that special person who is meant to bring them happiness and peace, designed especially for you, by your way of understanding the world.

You can get lost on that route you were meant to have all that you love, so bad you can remain with no idea of what you were. Especially when you haven't understood yourself well, you have to find a place which is where you belong, where so much that you are is appreciated. Unlike how we wander towards achieving our goals, and everything just falls apart from that. To be happy begins with finding your world, and everything that you discover from that will mean that much to you.

There's a place we're all meant to be, you can try to fit in somewhere, it just wouldn't work, and it can happen with so much that we engage in. Only to find that it doesn't align with who you are, or life itself, everything that you do just doesn't belong in that area of understanding. Even if you feel like you can adjust or adapt is part of those things you cannot change. On the other hand there's that time when you've arrived where so much that you are begins to make sense, and whatever you do is producing results of success.

Now that we want a lot out of life, as well as love, things become a little bit hard to understand, as we fail to get things right, and when you seek for someone who cares about you. Only to find that so much is still holding you back, and relationships don't need those kind of ups and downs, and is hard for one to commit to it. Whatever you are is not formed presently, and has excluded you from everything that is going on outside your world. So how do you work around that to find a solution to become what you want, as you cannot remain alone or let darkness fill your universe forever.

There are so many reasons why one may not form part of a certain world, which could be something you've already decided on becoming. You could have chosen a specific route to travel through which might be heading to your heart's deepest desires and you not there now, or you could've identified yourself with different types of human beings. Only to find that you live in separate spheres of life, and you don't see each other the way you should.

You need to ask yourself, where does your idea belongs? As so much that we call life is not meant for so many, and we get lost right from the beginning. You just become something which is not meant for everyone and from there you lose everything there is to live for, and instead of becoming what you will be happy with. You turn to what is for you to suffer, and moving ahead a lot becomes a sacrifice, and injure a pain of lacking joy which you cannot come to terms with, and love isn't there anymore.

It could be that to be happy you need to find someone who can exchange all that they are with you. By allowing you to enter into their lives without holding anything back, and giving you the best kind of love that has no boundaries. Therefore letting you in a chance to indulge in being together and sharing that special gift of life, and makes you forget the pain of what we know. As we die spiritually knowing so much, and you can hardly ever have peace from what you went through, and only true love has power to restore our well-being to normal.

If you truly have values, you will not only value your goals of success, you understand how to create a room for true love as well as that individual who makes what we are a reality. Our desires out of life can keep consuming so much in us, especially in situations where it has led to neglecting our responsibilities. Happiness doesn't come easy, and you know that as you could have once loved. It could be that now when you're so eager to achieve through your own creativity, it has taken over all that you are, and there is no enough time to give to everything.

You must fix your eyes on the value that someone possesses, without having to come back and settle for love as you could've been disappointed elsewhere. See through the simplicity of situations that life can present to you. Either way you wouldn't appreciate if things were extremely difficult, and that at the end doesn't mean you're meant for true love, and a solution to what you want to be.

When you are where you supposed to be and knowing what you doing that your attention is fully alert. You become aware of everything as it wouldn't be knowledge if it didn't teach you enough of what you must understand about what is valuable.

When you are within a certain path pursuing a very important goal it must let you into the center of knowledge where things are valued for what they're worth. So that even if you may have something given to you in a simple manner, you appreciate that which you're blessed with. As you know how it feels to be denied what you are, or really need, so take the love presented to you, as it doesn't matter how it has been offered to you, feel blessed, and hold it tenderly.

Beside that the suffering could've have lasted longer than it was meant to be, the thing could be that every moment of happiness feels like the easiest period we have ever been through in our lives. So is either you get used to the life you require to be happy or there will never be anything that you're grateful for.

If you want to learn the hard way or find out what something means. Then good will always be concealed from you, and you will never experience anything at its best. Arrive where you see the world the way it is, and know how valuable it means, as so much that came through your understanding must be valued as if is priceless.

A lot was always there, you just never attached any love to it, as you didn't feel it within you, only that when it was what you wanted, it communicated from deep within you. It meant so much that you lived to see it come to life, you bear the eager of witnessing something great, created by your own way of thinking. Yes it could have lasted longer, and now you have arrived at that period of understanding where you must accept that everything is real, and never look back.

Know that a heart ready to offer itself doesn't happen very often, it came when it was meant to be, you have been preparing yourself for it, and it became real. Is not about how many can play that role of fulfilling your need for happiness, is about who was willing to give themselves to you with kindness. Out of so many available one becomes enough, and everything to celebrate and be joyful about, is when you have arrived at that area where you truly fit in. As regardless of the world we see outside, there's where we belong and meant for the best from all that we desire, where love is true, and life is worthy.

How does it feels, now that you have arrived at that place where you had identified your success and everything you want to live for? Can you say that maybe there is something missing, given that at times is about opening one door that will lead to so many you wanted to walk through, and it does become worthy to live for?

We keep on increasing on that until is more, is a willing heart that persists on pushing, you hold on to what you love, and it becomes what you constantly pick up along the way. All of it will make up for your greatest ambitions, make the most of it as you not lucky to be there, you have worked hard and matured with situations.

So we feel lucky to have each other that the world has given us the opportunity to be together, and we love one another so much we don't ever want to look back, and we don't regret any moment of it. You know it wouldn't be easy to have met this kind of an individual, when someone has given themselves to you, and you admire how it has happened, that love just became a gift in every way possible. It feels right like your hearts were meant to be combined, and there's no argument about it, we never hope for something of this nature to come and be what we have.

Love comes to those who have it in them, and seek after it, the thing about life is that you can think less of yourself even when it comes to finding love. However your value has changed, and is no longer what you use to be. Now that you have find a purpose you have something in you that someone finds irresistible and that thing has brought true love to you, and it has made everything possible, and you thought that you didn't deserve. Maybe you do, you just hadn't given who you are appropriately, now that you did is time to receive the same back to you.

When you work for your ambitions, know that you mustn't lose yourself, as it does happen that you may become lost accidentally by failing to see where you headed. You could have started well, and never reached a point of deserving, or maybe is the kind of life that you're involved in that never gave you what you worth. Somehow it does exist and lies somewhere within you, what can turn our desires to something hard to achieve? It could be how we fail to focus at the center where love is the main theme, to all that we seek the most, we don't strive to reach that sense of belonging.

Through dedication in all of life's important concept your goals become easy to manifest, you just walk right into everything that you want. Even what you never hoped for, the secret is to remain faithful to what you deserve, true love does exist and we can find it. As hard as it could be to reach where it matters and truly valued, you can have it, and live it, if you have dedicated yourself in being the best with your heart fully longing for it.

Love is an invitation to a full happy life, where most of what you have prepared for has become a reality, and as much as you have felt how difficult things are. Through the union of hearts it has become easy, it takes strength to realize part of what you value mostly, and when you least expect it. You have arrived where everything that you deserve has become real. Unlike being stuck in a world that keeps taking away from you, and when you look time has passed and you haven't been given anything for who you are. It has consumed everything that you worth, without care for our values.

When love has been what you searching for, and hoping to achieve those deep connections with all your heart. Someone or something out there feels that calling and receives your hunger for life and it keeps on feeding you hope to get closer to what you yearning for. So make sure when you going out there that you not only aiming for monetary success as the reward. You have identified committing to that special person as well, as one of the most important things that will be very fulfilling.

Is not like you cannot find a partner to commit to now, is the quality that you will have at the end that matters. If you have worked for everything, you will have it where is truly worth all that you desired. Is when you have aimed at the goal with caring for another that it comes to be very simple.

Not that when you have failed to identify true love as your main objective, you can suffer lack of it, someone will come along. Now can it be true, and worth everything you wanted to live for, or complement the kind of personality you resemble, and reach at the level where you feel satisfied? Yet you can settle for whatever there is, as it is love and something has to give in as we are human. Still, according to the law of relationships you have failed to reach the balance, commitment must be balanced by the worthy we both possess towards each other.

When it has reached at that level, is love where is quality and it will give you that everlasting joy, meant for you to be happy. So how do you justify the kind of work that you must do, not knowing where you headed? While your mind should focus on the outcome of where you heading with this kind of lifestyle, being the way you will leave the rest of your life.

True communion is when you are made for each other, and you carried that value with you as long as you have lived. You felt the worthy of someone you needed to be with, who will come and fill that empty space in your heart, and you gave yourself to that course and lived happily ever after.

You mustn't head to the unknown, you keep moving with your heart aiming at finding true love. In a world hard to find the worth in something you remain focused, you identify so much with love from the beginning to the end. Happiness becomes the main motivation that has led you to that place, is not that you wouldn't have known how to be normal or common in society. It doesn't have to be something you carried the rest of your life, we all begin at that level where our minds were able to conceive what we want, until it developed into a very strong will we have on the inside.

Love must be stronger than all we have ever wished for, it must stand out, and becomes what must lead the way, and never allow anything to be what controls our destiny. It must be the deepest will we have for life, don't just hope that it will work itself out at the end. As it too does come with responsibilities, and it wouldn't hurt to have carried it along until you arrive at the right place.

Give in to it so much that it becomes the center of your goals, and is highly valued in everything that you desire, just don't plan so much and leave it behind, it will hurt you when you reach your goals, as it won't be there, and you might settle for whatever, while it could've matured with what you wanted.

You must travel all the way with everything that you want, and not to ever abandoned a single thing. For something else as it may feel good in the meantime, and overlooking what you are in the future. For a lot that you do don't forget the meaning you want to derive from life, and if you need to find happiness at the end. As nothing can ever have a happy ending, if it doesn't have love as the main theme in it. You can work hard and so much that you break barriers, only that if care wasn't there at the center of your focus, it has lost its connection with everything that is meaningful.

It must've been about all that matters the most through the ups and downs, from that point of departure you are required to attain every form of growth. The thing is that we grow where we valuable, in most of what we engage, we never knew where the way was headed.

We matured through the work we do every day, and besides that, slave for a lot of good to come to life as the main thing you value on that route, and the only important virtue; you hold with greatness closer to your heart. Be eager to see change in people's lives so that you can have the benefits of the goodness you have coming back to you, don't be selfish in every way possible, as that may turn you into someone lacking direction.

Touch lives in every turn that is the true magic to life, when you have done the best for people to find themselves within the context of your abilities. Their hearts will never rest until they see to it that you as well has achieved something that is truly magnificent and worthy in love. That part of your efforts will earn you the happiness you've been dreaming about. If is something that will provide for every need you have then don't regret giving everything you can to have it.

It will give you something that will mean the world to you, as you have given that much, if you believe you have potential, then it exists both ways, it can be used for good or bad. You can become selfish for money, and you can be in a hurry to have so much that you can look away from everything. Still, you must understand that we can't buy love, and again no matter what value you attach to it, a lot remains hidden from us.

It must have been what you earned from your dedication, as you will never know what someone has been doing for the rest of their lives. So true love become what you can't manipulate, you can only master situations, that kind of commitment became true through you.

True love if you feel the need to have it, you work for it, with all that you understand until you get to that level where your life is accepted by those who have purity in them. You don't give in, no matter how hard it becomes, you know you have more than your goals to value, and is part of everything you willing to sacrifice yourself for among all that you seek. When you realize that you have something of that nature to achieve, you behave accordingly. Appreciate the worth of what you love even before you arrive there, or have it, hold it closer to your heart.

Reserve a space for someone in you to understand how much you cared about who they are, before you even met them. As we can have goals, which is one thing, another thing which you might need to consider very well if you are to get there, is being in good shape. Be in a lovable condition so that one can take pride and joy in sharing their lives with you, as you must make where you need to be your first priority. Just don't forget to be sure of how you arrive there, where you want to be, the center of your love and focus.

As you continue on your journey, value human beings with all your heart, and never lose hope even on a single individual that you come closer to. Love a lot regardless of how disappointing some situation might be, let someone know how much they mean to you by continuously showing them that you care.

Now that true love is what matters the most, hold good and never let go, if something wasn't meant to be in your life. It will continue on that path of being unworthy, the value you have inside is what you get, people are worth being cherished, as you might never know who you mistreating.

You could be mistreating someone worthy of being cared for, and just like that true love has slipped away. People deserve all the goodness we have to offer, the thing about love is that we can never know who we committing to in real life. Nobody has an idea of what goes on behind closed doors, so the best thing is to prepare yourself, by doing good. Knowing that you are only investing in the worth that could come to exist, and that is by all means the only thing we hope that even if justice is hard to find, there it came to exist.

Even the truth doesn't seem to be of significant value until it gets to relationships, you can't tell whether someone is lying or not, at times if it is possible you might see. With love of all that exist, you can never know what it means, or tell the difference, is just for you to give yourself completely to it. Living by the faith you have hoping is what must be, we could have wondered about the need to have virtues that are meant for us to keep as a guide to life and moving forward, what are they at the end?

Is that they apply somewhere and that is in love, where they are the most important and precious possessions to have. All over our lives the use of them never feels adequate enough, they don't appear to play a very big role in anyone's life. People are disappearing with crimes, now can you get away with it when it comes to love? There it seem to be a part of our lives where we're cornered, you don't know the stranger you letting into your heart, and that's the most important need for it.

So where do you find that person who is worthy of everything you worked for, the heart you are, willing to attract the same out there. A good individual who is just meant to give you everything you need in a commitment, that regardless of the world you see out there. They have good stored in them, and we know that about ourselves, no matter how bad we have behaved. You hoping to find someone who is worthy of all the love that exist in a human being, and when that time to commit comes, you give everything thinking it will change situations.

Just that, it can never change a thing, if you have ruined the seed of true love in you then you will not reap the benefits of true commitment. If is quality you have in you, then it will be a devoted person that you get, and one can try to dress it up hoping that it will have a good appeal.

Only that is what lies underneath that make up for the people that we are, and that's where the truth is. Love is deep within us, is not clothed, or decorated, is just how it is, it doesn't change, it remains the same beyond everything that we can understand. So hope for it and that it must come to exist, and it will happen if you have given yourself to it.

How would you have known that you need to do everything for love? Maybe it is honesty, as so much does catch up with us at some point, and we can keep avoiding the truth all the way, only that you can never hide forever. Reality is so broad, whatever you running away from will always be coming after you, and we refuse to live with the crimes we have committed, and we pretend as if we not guilty. Just that in love is where it came down to be realized exactly how bad it is, as we live with so much that we don't do right.

We get over things easily and right there at that point of loving someone. It continues to linger, and that's where the punishment is equal to the crimes we have committed, and you are so surprised why it caught up with you. Of which is fairly understandable, is that thing which we cannot control about our lives, you just allow a criminal to walk into your life.

Only if you have seen the need to have realized how important it is, to reserve a space for someone. Then love would have never failed you, it would have been perfect, it will come to be through the good you have in your heart.

Is the kind of thing you will find hard to understand, if you have never experienced it, there must be grounds for love and commitment, for things to come and make sense in our lives. You have to pray and hope for something which is what you know is true about life, you might not be sure of what makes everything a reality. Still, have faith in what you know which is what you've become over time, and in the loving heart you have inside, and what you have worked hard for. Everything that is happening outside the cycle of true love is the only place where a lot isn't real.

So much can happen according to your believes and the faith you have inside, though in love you have to admit to yourself, things did take you by surprise. You did experience something which you were not sure about, is where a lot catches up with us, and everything is there when you have worked for it. Do not hope to find anything except that true love which you seek knowing is what you have invested in, and is how you have hoped it would be. You gave yourself for it to happen like it did, and it was the only thing that became real about life.

Chapter Nine

Breakdown

There are so many reasons why a human being reaches at that point whereby they can't do it anymore. Regardless of how well one has been doing, they just stop trying, and it comes at a certain time where a lot is expected of someone and you just don't have that eager no more.

No matter how hard you try you just keep going to that place where you hurting, you not coping with situations, and that's how it all start. With a broken heart or a disappointment, and are those kind of situations which we can try to run away from, at times you can never know what could go wrong.

It could emerge from anything, the loss of a valuable entity, and most of it is trust. When you believe in someone or something so much that you just give all that you have and you don't want to know what could stand in your way. Yes is only natural that when everything is right, you cannot deny yourself a chance to be happy. Then it happens along the way that no matter how joyful you are, a certain thing just goes wrong and regardless of how hard you try you cannot go back to that state of complete happiness.

Some are situations that you can try to look away from, whereas with others you can't, they are meant for you to face them, and it can happen at any point in your life that the only person you have ever trusted disappoints you. Regardless of what you could have done, they just don't want to be part of you anymore, and the issue that you facing cannot be justified by anything. As people we take disappointments in different ways, to some it could be easy to once again start where they left off.

Whereas some can be affected deeply that they refuse to ever commit. You become so scared of what has happened so bad it doesn't feel like you can ever be happy again, and you ask yourself countless questions, of when you will be able to find someone, who can give you what they are.

Love has a huge effect on all of us, and it can happen, that you loved someone so much, only that now they're just not interested in you any more, or how you wanted one to feel about you, and you can't tell when one is lying or telling the truth. Although you can swear that at some point that it was true love you had, something just got in the way.

It could have been love once, now is no longer there, and you're all alone. What can you be without the one you had loved deeply and with dedication that you had given all that you are to them, and without knowing what could've gone wrong, you just not meant for each other anymore? And not having to mention so much, that effect of losing someone you know is capable of tearing a human soul apart, and we are never prepared enough for this kind of a thing.

Now that we're never ready for this kind of situations, you just give yourself completely, and you cannot know what someone can do. Since as human beings we differ so much in behaviour, and to what makes us who we are, or what we can do on the other side, and if the other fails to be trustworthy.

That changes the nature of everything that we doing, and nothing can ever stay in the dark, some things are meant to show, and when it comes out, it doesn't only affect one. Both parties become so deeply affected by it, to a level where they can even fail to move forward with their lives.

Love is supposed to bring us happiness, when is now failing to produce that kind of outcome, you ask yourself, what am I to do with myself? As some are not just lovers, are human beings who overtime have become our shelters, home, as well as refugees. The only place we have to lean on for everything we need, and now you have to live without that individual, and when that kind of situation has occurred, you don't know where to go for anything.

We trust so much with human beings that you just give someone your whole heart, and when something goes wrong, you fail to adjust to the changes that you going through. You become too broken to adapt to situations, and you remain there lingering in pain, and without a clue how to face a new day coming to exist.

Love has that power to take away so much that we value inside and outside. Is the only thing capable of working you to a level so low you can't remember where you are, or who to trust any more, and it can consume so much from human beings, and leave us with nothing to live for.

As innocent as we can be, or how exciting relationships can feel, you could have never predicted what could ruin the spark of love that existed between two people who felt belonging to each other. That is the thing, we give ourselves to human beings we don't even know what they're capable of. Worse for a very long time they make you believe as if something existed and you pass those premature stages until you hooked in completely.

As much as we are looking for happiness, you cannot deny yourself an opportunity to be happy even if not all the time, for those few convincing moments, inside our soul they lasted forever, and it happens at the end that what you got out of it, is not the complete joy you wanted.

This is regardless of how someone must value another person's presence in their lives. So much can happen which was not meant to and that slowly destroys everything you worked hard for, and you could have seen human beings, and thought that it can never happen to you. Now it has happened and you were not prepared for it, at times is not like we are really heart broken, and is to be shocked.

You become so surprised at what one can do to another after promising to love you against all odds, and we never set grounds or barriers for commitments. We feel free to give completely what we are, which is our most valuable possession, and before you know it a lot that you are has disappeared and there's nothing to live for any more.

Is not about what you can do from there on, is what you think of yourself and what you might resent to, as a way of dealing with your emotions, compared to moving along with life normally. A lot of things feels like we doing them on purpose, whereas we could have been pushed a little bit to be at that stage where we neglect ourselves.

As we are made different, how you handle the pain inside truly proves the kind of individual that you are. You may feel like you don't need to trust any more or you continue with life knowing that in your heart you have no need to give yourself to anyone.

When the heart refuses to open up to another you might give yourself to so much which isn't love, as you lack that virtue of true love which is trust. You don't have faith to let someone be in your life, or allow the other to rely on you, and you might live in denial of the situation and how it has happened. The truth is, that's where you broke down, you failing to admit it to yourself that is where you lost everything, and now you are on a journey living without a purpose to move forward.

That is beside what life on its own can do to an individual when you've misunderstood things. You can lose a lot and your focus to progress normally, and part of that can happen at any stage, and you just give up like that. To be content we balance ourselves with so much, and anything can steal that first love we have for everything.

If you don't ever understand what you were meant to do on your own, for a very long time you can remain in the mist of impossible situation. It does happen regardless of how you feel or what you know, that without a well define purpose that drives you from within, you feel miserable, as you lack a path to channel your energy.

When all that you are is been strongly questioned by situations you facing, is only through a definite goal in mind, that you are able to face those kind of obstacles you encounter on a daily basis.

Whenever something tries to get you down, you are able to respond to it based on what you understand about life. Now when you've failed to acquire knowledge of anything that exist outside your natural logic. What are you supposed to do with yourself, or with all that you are when you can't even make sense of whatever you see in a positive manner?

Can a purpose to be what we truly desire be enough to give us strength not to succumb to anything along the way, regardless of how we feel challenged? What we aiming at becomes our frame of reference, your mind has power to think independently, no matter what situations can be pulling you to become.

Especially when you have allowed the goal to be what drives you onwards, things only begin to make sense when you have passed through your faith and your way is no longer heading backward. You fully understand what you are and what you need to do to reach your full potential, and you are settled whatever comes your way.

Knowing very well that deep in your thoughts you looking at ways on how to grow towards manifesting your own thinking. You become so formed that whatever threatens you doesn't change a thing that you are. So when that isn't there, what will you become when faced with the toughest obstacles you have ever met? We need to have a way to deal with situations that we encounter on a daily basis. Your understanding in the world is your reservoir of energy, where you draw the strength necessary to face every day.

So when you prepare for life, though you not familiar with why you should be doing so. Make sure you work very hard to gather enough strength necessary to pass through everything. As you will never know when you might need it to get ahead, for every challenge can turn to be the most difficult we have ever faced.

Even if we cannot understand so much, yet that knowledge of what now forms you becomes a fortress, when you've striven to stretch your horizon. As we cannot predict what lies ahead of the way we traveling, and failure to have thoroughly look ahead can result in a setback.

As we cultivate our faith in the right direction, our minds becomes fully motivated in terms of holding on to a meaningful way that is focused on happiness. As anything can happen to steal away that tender we have, given that you can never know the results of everything you do.

So much that we engage in slowly challenges life and for one to fall into traps, and without knowing what has happened something comes and changes all you've ever known or loved. So whatever we see out there is not meant for us to understand or last if we haven't passed through ourselves first, we are mostly created by what we need to reach for.

What will you do when you discover that so much out there is not design for you to understand what you are unless you're discipline? And you cannot be part of it without creating your own perspective. As we move through so much that we've seen over the years, which later becomes our point of contact, and is how you analyses the kind of knowledge that will brighten up your future. It can become the light or it can darken our lives all over ourselves, and from that you can either feel pushed or easily accepted to be part of life.

It proves how much we are our own solutions towards everything that we love. Even the closest people we have cannot be what we really need from deep within to be at our full potential. We treasure our own lives, if it was something else you struggling with so many could be able to give you hope.

So when you failing to find a meaningful concept and a purpose which can light up your world, leaves everyone powerless. When you find that inner light nothing can ever be a situation you cannot work out on your own. You have become the pillar in you, and nothing is stopping you from engaging with your soul and become what you know is your deepest desire.

You could have lived, and so far you haven't find the love for everything that is life, as it is right now you still suffer the most common signs of depression, from not being content. You know that you don't have it in you to see the way, and that's what it does to us in most instances when you still struggling with discovering which way to travel.

You lost your purpose in that place which could be the beginning of all that you are. As we growing up moving forward with everything, and without being prepared you have made a little progress, you came across a certain area where so much just became too much to handle.

You failing to reach that inner person who is there to help you thrive through adversaries, and without that side of yourself. You become weak to see what you should be doing, and it happens that is within a period of your life where you need to know where the way is headed, and you just can't understand anything. We have so much that stands against us and at some point it can find you unprepared for everything, which could be worse, and it could be difficult to ever cope with situations.

Without a well-defined purpose you can get lost so much that whatever comes in your path is meant to pull you to whichever direction, and with no need to mention what could be the solution.

Is having to stand firm with understanding that could be the only way to be content, and for what is worth you haven't reached there now, and what you know about the world is not enough to show you the route forward. You can become confused in any stage of your life, it could be at a point where you are not sure of what you doing, and you could have the idea and not know which road to take.

As you struggle with understanding so much just comes down hard on you, when you get to see what you doing, you begin to realize that is not the future that you battling with.

Is the past that has that much effect on you, how you got stuck there, when certainly everything that we are catches up with us, and it refuses for one to move on with life. That it requires for you to remain there, and fix that part of yourself, then you can think of advancing to the next level. As we are all born with a gift of knowing how to work out the solution to a lot that we're faced with.

You have reached that point where you not down, to recognize that certain things could be wrong with your life. Only that you cannot move forward either, and it requires that you take your time and look into it.

You just have to attend to the person that you are on the inside and work it out on your own, surely there's no one who can help you see the way if is not there in you. Is you who stop lingering in that place where you are, whether something is not right with you or you just need a new beginning, you can be the only solution that you require.

What makes it worse, once something dies you cannot make it live again, you just disappear with it, and for you to come back you could need more than you can give to your own self. The only thing to understand is what could've led to that point where you are found stuck, as goals and dreams are one thing, and relationships can have another effect on you as well. You must pay attention to everything carefully, as you can never know which part is it that has collapsed, even so, love more than life is the pillar of it all.

If you have love you cannot resent yourself to that level where you can't figure out the way to move forward. Now that we human beings who live in and out of relationships, the devil can come at any point in our lives, where you are in between your best moments. Maybe you just went out of a certain commitment, or now that we cannot be focused on being with someone alone. It happens that you need to know which direction to take to discover more about you, as you need to make a living as well.

So much comes in and out of our lives with different impact and you don't know what the next person can be as a sort of an effect on you. Right there in that very moment you just become broken if you haven't built faith in yourself. You need to fix your eyes on the way forward through a certain thing which becomes the greatest pillar of all, that even if love disappears you remain content, and what you have to figure out is who to trust.

As we pick up a lot in every corner of our lives, and that could be the problem, you could end up taking part of what you don't align with. You need to know precisely what is it that you want to do with passion, as you could be a person living a very satisfactory life, however something could be there which can weaken you severely.

More like once in our lives we go through that period where we have to prepare ourselves for the kind of people we want to be. Of which part of that life entails having to endure so much to resemble the character where you are able to handle whatever comes your way, and is part of the person that you are. Whether you heading the corporate way, to the stars, or you just want to have a perfect family, you need to be well groomed for everything, as you will come across people.

You will deal with a lot of human beings who are different or rather difficult, and your family as well. Need that much understanding from you and it all became possible, given that even on your own you were able to pass whatever could stand in your way, and that's the results of the kind of life we see on a daily basis.

People equipped with the skills to handle every problem that they encounter, is like we go through that gate of intellectual capacity that changes us into very strong individuals. From there we are never the same to what we use to be, and we are well prepared for everything, and what we love the most.

So you cannot avoid it, and I guess on the other hand you can say that we are given as much as we require from this world. Just that we have to deserve it to acquire it, as it could happen that whatever challenges we face are our own tests. We are being tested to see how far we're capable of understanding things. What role can we play, and part of that will be our heritage forever, and you need to own it, you claim it, or take what's yours out of this universe. So the adversaries we go through are meant to reveal our true identity.

We all have that thing standing before everything we love, which can push you beyond this world, and it can question your intellectual understanding, to see what you're capable of. Do we understand our whole lives, are we those kind of people that are worthy of being treasured forever, or soon along the way you will give up, or maybe you can never try at all?

You will eventually stop trying right there at that beginning of your life. You just throw everything away and say is not meant for me, I cannot do it anymore, and now your fate can be decided by any situation that you come across.

Is so amazing when you get to realize how good it is that we have so much that we need, right at our disposal. You have the opportunity to be whatever you want, and that is one thing good about this world, that no matter what you go through is nothing compared to the life that you will live.

Only that we have a period once in our lives ready to steal all that we value, and questions everything that we are, and you can never run away from it. To escape from it is to avoid our responsibility to be human which you don't have to, so you get to choose how far you want to matter.

How far do you want to grow, do you want to reach at that level where you live a complete life? Is all there, and for you is to make up your mind about it, and what you want to be. Whether you need a plan or maybe you don't, you cannot have part of your destiny decided for you, and this are some of the things that can really get you down.

When you're required to look for yourself where you don't even know what to be any more, and so much can turn to be difficult when it has to be you who must figure out your way about what you must become.

Although we have so much decided for us, and now that we want more out of this world, it all depends on you and what you understand, and a lot is there. You have a choice to choose exactly how you want to live your life, and once you have the will, the way will follow, and nothing is stopping you.

Though at some point, having to handle your responsibilities, and needing to think about what you want can be a little difficult, as we are not meant for everything. Some things you will know, while others you won't, more like we have the same path to travel and you get to select what you want to be for yourself.

Is what we choose that we get to be, and regardless of the fact that we can have our lives thought for us. In the path we have chosen for ourselves we get to do our own thinking for our well-being, and if you insist on being what you have decided for yourself; how will you know where you going or what to do, or if you will ever reach that place?

As we have so much given, more like we are bought out of everything. When you decide to become a regular person living a standard life, keen on serving someone or the interest of an organization, you have been taken out of so much.

In that case we can say that the stress is taken off your shoulders and have a plan that was well done given to you, you're taken care of everywhere you have needs, so you don't apply your mind. All that you needed is to have served, and that is so as the world constantly tries to improve life for humanity to be better.

Value is created so that we can have more, or maybe invented by someone who understand everything regarding people's lives. As that's what we do, we share our experiences with each other, and what you need is to have played your role, do your part, and make sure that you meet the requirements.

So life would've been that we're required to think everything for ourselves, now that so much which people get to suffer from, has become an opportunity to do business. A lot of what we were meant to understand has been done for us, and we are just left with those minor roles that we must play as a means to be human or if necessary.

Like the need to have been educated can lead you to that perfect job where there are a lot of benefits, and to make sure that all is taken care of. People have decided to cover everything so that our complete needs are catered for, and you're able to focus on serving your duties.

Now that everything is about serving the ordinary path and be taken care of, but you want to be a star, and stand out. You live to do something amazing with your life, you don't have anything thought for, you decide your own success, your fate is in your hands, and you have no one to put your faith on. All your plans are in your mind, as regardless of how much they can offer us, we still believe in ourselves, and that we can do incredible things through our own understanding.

So you believe in the goal, and right there at the beginning you have decided that everything about you is making it happen beyond what so many can understand, and now that ideas begin somewhere. You have the concept however you don't know how to put it out there, you are at that point where you want to find a meaning to derive, and beside the vision, you stuck at which path to follow precisely.

Now that you have to work on the plan by yourself, or do everything on your own, and make sure is a life that will give you so much that you require out of this beautiful world, and is what you love.

Not knowing what to do might stress you a little bit, until you figure out which way to go. It can happen at the initial stage of your journey that you feel lost, and it could be that you need to value your options. You have to choose what is best for you, and be certain is the kind of life or love that you deserve, as there are no benefits for all our needs, you have to work for it to be worthy.

So don't forget to put your deepest desire first, to be able to find a way on how to achieve it. For it to be what drives you onwards in what you do, as there won't be any miracles to come and deliver what you long for. So you cannot overlook the need to figure out so much for yourself, and make sure whatever path you follow the outcome is what will make you happy.

Even though the route might be difficult to find, still, you need to be sure you traveling through a way that will give you so much that you deserve. So true love could be something hard to achieve, and if you choose to travel through its path, you might get everything you looking for. Given that no matter what you serve, love come to those who are worthy, and is not about what another can offer.

Is you who pulls everything that you meant for, when you have worked hard. One can try to dress it up, or someone can be there where they need to be, at the end is the heart that matters. We always attract what we are, and you can never know what a person could be, even so, your soul will find its mate.

Chapter Ten

Focus Ahead

We have so much pulling us sideways, to whichever direction that feels like life, and it doesn't make any sense, you can choose to either focus on it, or you can pay attention to what you love. The thing is that there will forever be something to destruct you, and for all that is worth, whatever comes in that nature, will always be after some precious possession within us. It could be anything that you value, which can get the better of you, although there are those that hurt the most, which if you don't look carefully you can fall prey to.

Once you find yourself stuck in that kind of situation, you become affected all over your life, and immediately people realize that there are those things that touches us where we fragile. They start capitalizing on that, mostly what could get the better of us is love, when it isn't true, it can weigh you down so much. At some point you can feel like it is better being alone than having to put up with something that you know so well isn't healing you, or creating the person you want to be.

Love hurts and can create severe depression, so bad that if you haven't learned to be discipline. You can feel like someone is doing it intentionally just to hurt you, or push you to resent yourself to something unworthy of who you are.

Although there is so much that can affect a person, there is what stands out above everything, and is there to get you down.

So much that can get the better of us, are things which are meant to slow our progress of life moving towards a good direction and success, or you can at times try to overlook all that is happening around you. Be someone worthy of the life they live, and learn to value your own understanding and create a path that will get you where you want to. You clear your heart and your head of all that exists out there so that you can value what you are within, and let go of so much which doesn't even make up for the reality you have created in you.

If you not sure of which path to follow, you may feel like someone is holding the part which you are specifically dependent on to move forward clearly, and they're not. So much that you require to advance further with life is always depending on you with what you know. You let go of all outside influences, and focus on your passion, if you have find one, and not to build reliability on something that require people's input, and which constantly disappoints you, that cannot give you what you need.

If you there, things are about what you know, which became a way through you, that's how you accomplish freedom from everything happening around you. To create your own understanding is something meant to set one free and achieve complete happiness. You look away from so much which is there to hold you back, or what opposes all that you are.

To find your true calling you might need to sort out all the misunderstandings arising from the outside world, and focus on creating a brighter perspective. Which could be better at enlarging your vision to see on a bigger picture. As there are a lot of things which exists that can confuse someone when you have failed to make sense of the reality we live in, until you end up in places you've never thought of.

Only to realize later that you've been delayed and held back in so much. It would make a lot of difference if everything was there to equip you in becoming a good person. Now when you're not been channeled through the right direction, what would you do? Or look at everything that is happening and say that you understand what you are.

The part of life where you can go through so much, which isn't what you are happy about or what you wanted can destroy a lot that you value. You can pick up things which are not necessary for what you aiming at, you know who you are and what you want out of this world.

Now when you go through the troubles of being pulled back or sideways, ask yourself, what are you learning from such situations? Are you being groomed towards your destiny, and if not, how do you recover from those kind of setbacks? And it happens all the time that when you're not where you love about life, you live to force things to manifest.

When you have found your passion everything seems to be easy, you become a burning flame of enthusiasm and nothing can hold you back. So much only means that we are caught up in that period of our lives where we are not sure about what we doing, and we keep succumbing to people's ideas. A clear purpose will not allow anything to hold you down, if you by any chance feel delayed, so much of you still depend on outside factors.

You can find yourself wasting time on so much which you know very well doesn't serve you, and you might think is meant to be. At times you didn't need all that you became along the way and you could have traveled a straight path. What you needed was a well-defined objective to your deepest desire, so if you somehow are still holding on to what you were in the past. It means you haven't discovered anything to be happy about, or a meaningful purpose in the future, you keep trying whereas you not passing.

You can lose who you are, as you were something special to yourself, you are what got you traveling in this path. At least that was enough to give you the drive towards a better direction, and it might feel like you will remain the same. This way of life is meant for those who have faith, and are so eager to see change in their lives. Who are holding on to their own ideas, and have become the answer to their problems.

To have discovered what you passionate about increases your confidence, unlike finding yourself stuck in between different worlds. You become very distracted and fail to connect with all of life, whenever something feels like too much to understand, you know where to look for answers. As you have found that purpose which you needed to remain deeply focused or hooked towards success, and you could've been going on normally when you changed your way.

As what you were was not serving your inner goal and it disappeared from that. You could have been living a life you were not sure about, and as much as you doubted what you are or what you knew. Now you must find a new direction, is not that what you are wasn't necessary, it could have been that you didn't believe in yourself as you needed to. Hence you couldn't find the significance that it serves, you failed to discover a purpose in what you use to be.

Now the question you should constantly ask yourself is; are you still struggling with understanding what you need to be, is it hard to find a way to be something you really love? If you haven't decided on what you yearn most, so much could be difficult to make sense, if what you were hasn't worked well. You have to learn a new way, which will arouse your passion, and with no doubt what you are will find meaning from that, if what you used to be has no place in your life any more.

So imagine if you had allowed situations which you didn't know what they are, or which you cannot control to rule your life, that you opened a way for so much to pass. You failed to grasp your destiny, as regardless of whether we believe it or not, our lives are meant for greatness.

If you still have faith or the will to be human, you were born to be successful and be something special and you know you cannot resent yourself like that, and it teaches us about value. We have to treasure every moment that we live and be creating a lot of good with our time.

Things would make a lot of sense if one has permanently defined what they love about life, and how far their willing to go to make that a reality. How devoted you are to that, how wide do you want to spread your wings through that value you carrying that has become like a virtue, that needs you to hold on to.

So to be sure that no matter what the world does this part of you is not something that you must let go, and you learn by all means to be faithful to that promise which you have made to yourself. As we cannot acquire knowledge after so much has passed, what an opportunity it would have been, as the vision opens our eyes to seize any chance that presents itself.

Although what we know is not the same as what we become through our own understanding, knowledge defines what we were supposed to be through a literary way of life. On the other hand there's what you are, which is what you think, or part of what you invented in your head, you saw a purpose to serve which aligned with what you love and it felt right for you. It could've been a thought that began in your mind and now it has become what drives you towards the future. Is something that becomes enough for all that we wanted to be, and fits into context of the passion we have for everything.

Maybe where you were was the right place to be, is just that you couldn't have things easily, as the path was not motivating enough to reach your full potential. You felt pushed to begin something which will bring out the love in you, and instead of feeling sacrificed to find meaning out of life. You felt overwhelmed to be gaining more understanding, and turning that into a lot of good became worthy of who you are.

To see your own ideas becoming concrete foundation to everything that you wanted to live for, and though it could have been painful having to think so much to the end, through your own knowledge. Still, if you ever succeed so much becomes easy to have.

All that you have ever imagined could be able to come alive, even if you go through so much along the way, the outcome of that feels worthy of the path you traveled. While at some point you may think about the knowledge you had which you abandoned, you somehow accept the transformation.

You could have been something where you possessed that kind of understanding, but overlooked that window of opportunity for passion to form into your life. Regardless of how we feel as it is a journey to worthiness, and is worth embracing and for those who will sacrifice what they use to be for it, they will have fullness in their hearts.

Situation could have been normal, yet that calling for something so fulfilling spoke directly to your heart. It called you into creativity, and now you must work on this life where the goal is to find your passion and be happy about it. As it will create everything that you value, and so many can only realize that after it has passed, how they could've been their greatest invention.

You wasted time on something which never repaid you for all your efforts, and you haven't benefited as much as you have given. How can you recover from such a setback? Knowing that time can have a huge hold on you, or can never be reversed.

So you stick to what you have found to be the answer to all that you ever wanted, as that might be able to lead you to what you yearning for. As so much could be very confusing if you haven't decided what you are, you let go of that which exists outside the law of life and love, and focus on what is your deepest desire, and true ambition for everything.

As we have a lot that we don't do for ourselves, we live to be accepted, still, you don't need any body's approval if isn't going to make you happy on the inside, or impress anyone outside the destiny of being yourself. See your star and head for it, as that would be the only satisfaction you get from this world.

You can find yourself traveling a path you have never known, just by making a mistake which you could have avoided with the life you desire, and that can never be undone. As we are all given equal chances to do what we want, when time pass, it passes with everything we value.

Which is who you are where you could've had so much that you love. You have to choose something that will give you what you've always needed on time, or you can never make peace with it. In the near future or at the end there must be a fulfilling answer to the kind of person you have chosen to become.

Yes it takes so much out of a human being to find new meaning and closure with what has passed. However deep within we all possess that thing which can lead us to a new and a brighter future, which you are capable of. As failure to have discovered that about your life could reflect like you have failed, the end mustn't be that you are disappointed.

It must be about how you got delayed and made it, very big, and produced that sense of satisfaction, and be able to make peace with the time you have lost. How would you justify that to yourself if you never reach what you were looking for?

In order to find happiness, do we insist on following something bigger than what we can easily understand, which is who we are, regardless of what situations and time can do to us? Do you live with the believe that there's what we are meant to be and to get there we keep traveling through ways we haven't known? Which in doing so we lose so much and part of what we were, and if you never look back or regret what you use to be you becoming a new human being.

You let go of so much that only through a realized goal in the future your life can begin to make sense again, and regardless of what you engage in, we all can go through such situations. So if you have allowed the desire to be what drives you, know you growing towards a greater purpose, and the more you are willing to let go of what you were. The better you have opened your heart to accept something new about yourself, as that is a reflection of faith.

To pass through such situations you are required to have reflected all kinds of virtues necessary for what you want. More like we are born constructed in a way which is meant for a certain life, and through that path we could've reached where we would have been happy with our lives. When you felt that you don't normally fit in within that context, you saw a need for a change into something better.

Now that we just dream it, whereas we don't know how far we supposed to have prepared for it, you came across that challenge requiring that you give in completely, and never tire, as you will not know how much is enough for what you now want to become.

As much as we're not failures you will reach at that level where you achieve what you love through your own understanding, and then you begin to free yourself from the past life you had. As it happens that when you seek for a change you felt unworthy of the person that you were, and now that you cannot be without anything to hold on to, you remained with the old self.

Since you couldn't be vain, and needed something to make you a human. As you had become tired of the former being, and until you arrive at your new destiny that's what you had, and regardless of how much you hate who you were, you can't escape that unless is by a virtue of the path you have identified.

Though it can never happen easily, something will eventually give in to what you are, that is regardless of how you can feel undeserving of all that is life. Beside that we are meant for more, so much can keep refusing the person that you are, as your understanding isn't adequate for now. Still, if is happiness you seeking there has to be what accepts you for everything that you know, given that as people we differ somewhere so deep and with a lot that we do.

You can never know that what you are will be worthy and enough for as much as you want, and you need to try hard and with your ultimate faith. As is sad that you cannot be what you want out there, somewhere you will feel left out. There are just those boundaries that permanently say that we are not meant for every form of existence.

Part of us is contagious and can be involved in so much that there is, only to find that somethings just becomes a different world. Even if you can try to relate there's no relationship there, and that's why we need to be careful all the time to be permanently focused on what we know we good at.

As there could be those type of acts that can hold you back forever, activities that don't belong in our lives, and somehow we can find ourselves involved in it. Is when you envy something that you know is life for so many, and unfortunately is not meant for you. We cannot be doing everything that exists, some things are not what you can understand and you have to make peace with that.

So don't be broken when you realize how limited we are at times, and focus on the part of life which you good at, and never tire of going deeper as more will keep revealing itself as we go on. So feel comfortable in that part of creation where you exchange who you are and what you good at. As so much that we keep bringing to our lives is there to dehydrate us, and we strain severely.

So do likewise and focus straight ahead, leave all that which could be meant to hold you back from progressing to success. As we go through these kinds of situations every day, that seeks to weigh us down, and you might need to resist the temptation.

You are being weighed down by something that could be anything and unworthy of your efforts. To be really specific, what is meant for us to pay attention to and what isn't for us to entertain? And how do you know that this is for you as you can never tell if something is worth the while until you're standing there at the end, and see the results it has brought to your life. Maybe is honesty as we all know how capable we are and where we're failures.

If something is worthwhile, it must be meant to last forever, if it cannot get you to the end of your life, knowing that you brought love for that particular thing. Then there's no need to waste all your time on that specific aspect of your understanding. What would you become when it can no longer carry you through the journey you've begun? It must be enough to pull you out of the hardships and setbacks which one can face in a lifetime.

You can try to live in denial holding on to something which doesn't serve you any more, while you know is true. Where you pause your life to think about what you are, it must be from the beginning to the end. Otherwise there's really no need, and nothing can justify one's efforts standing there watching so much passing by for some time. While you know you have an obligation to get up and do everything with the time that you have.

Complete devotion is the birth of a true star, our desires comes to life through such efforts of dedication in what you know how to do. When is born in you, it must be prepared for the rest of its existence. All of which you go through is nothing except life's obstacles to the end of everything that you doing.

Time might have passed while you remain in that place, and whatever could have trapped you in that kind of situation can refuse to let go of you. Only that transformation towards reaching your destiny will allow you to pass through that, and conquer your fears.

Now from all that you striving to become you must be getting somewhere, as there are important parts of life which you may suffocate from, like love. Otherwise we are always capable of carrying ourselves wherever we go, and understand that when you see people moving in together, they have the means to remain as one. Nothing can ever separate them, is lack that divide human beings to be single. As you begin to feel the strain of not being where you must be, know that so much that you going through is meant for you alone.

You could have had your way with relationships, now in this new life trying to achieve the best that you can. You will feel the need to stand aside and watch human beings be involved with each other for some time, and they will do it. As love waits for no one, if you not there you cannot be part of that cycle of true love, which is what you seek, and you not valuable to all that there is now. You can wander trying to justify that your needs are not satisfied, whereas is you who never fulfilled the need to be human currently understanding what matters most.

You can be afraid, and yes be very scared of everything that can go wrong, who can pretend like they're blind to see that you not coping with things. All the needs you fail to satisfy they take away something vital to being a normal human, and you can keep on hanging there thinking that it will be easy for someone to be part of your life, and is not. Everybody has status and reputation, and it has nothing to do with what you want to be or whom you think you are, it is about the person that you are right now, not on the inside or in the future.

Deep within, you have the knowledge and you know who you are and what you deserve, and when you haven't done things right, you denying your life what you entitled to. You can try to feel better and convince yourself, it wasn't meant for you, and that can be very hard on you when you have to let go of all that you worthy of.

While settling for less isn't the answer either, as it is there in you, it could be that you not living it, and you can pretend like you didn't know. Still, somewhere inside it pains you as bad as you understand everything there is about true value and love.

If one has never known so much is better you're not being denied anything, as you haven't experienced a lot that this life has to offer. The pain lingers in you who has paused their normal progress for something to come into being. Whereas you had been happy elsewhere and there was plenty that you loved and you abandoned all that. Do we have to do everything that we love, or maybe strive to reach our desired goals, or you cannot risk not going through with your objectives unless you're prepared to succeed?

The person that you are inside that you have been reserving is you as well, and you require that part of who you are. It could be that you haven't been born in the world and it is the transformed version of you. Maybe that is what you were in the past, and you got bored of that life, as monotony is not the only way to live. There is a constant need for a change and accept a different part of your understanding, and you can't live with yourself unless you become this new being that you're anxious to be.

With a clear purpose at heart is only a matter of time before you're ready to come back to being a normal person, and despite what is going on around you. Do you believe that you exist inside where you know what you doing? And part of you currently live to find your essence, and it has become the only reason why you had to sacrifice yourself, and though so much tries to drag you down. Within you are very convinced on becoming this new being, regardless of how sad so much can make you feel, as in the current version, you not what you love about you.

In your vision, you have achieved better than you need to, more like you couldn't settle for all that people are. You needed something more fulfilling, and very rewarding to what you currently have. How can you refuse what is present about us human beings, and look for a greater life, even if for a very long time you choosing to go without everything vital to being a valid individual now.

How many people walk with it, from when the sun comes up until it dawns? Knowing that life would have been better, yet for now, things can stop just a little bit as there's a need for something else which will be a way to acquire more as a human being.

We want so much out of this world, and is necessary for us to have those kind of things, still, why abandoned the present, as it must be the ultimate purpose, to all that we deserve. If we don't get up immediately and act on it while we thinking about it, would it ever matter, as time will not always be on our side.

When time has passed, and what we have known has become insignificant or you no longer fit in the world of commonest and you have nothing left. Can you cope with situations around you? As a normal life would have made a lot of sense, for the present is always the right time. We look away or leave all behind and get up there and do something with our lives and be common in society, instead of trying hard to stand out. What if you fail, and you look back at the clock only to find that it has elapsed further than you have ever imagine or can handle?

It does happen that you can find people struggling with something at a very late age knowing very well that time is not on their side. It has begun declining, and you can try to say good about such a situation, and there's no great there, once the clock has begun to run out, start racing. Is better here at your early age where you still have so much to offer, and if there was nothing you could be or involved in and there's not much you holding back on, then don't give up.

Give it all that you got and become something special. You could have been so many things and you chose to be what you are currently, and life would have been better and maybe you might have done wonderful things with your time. Just that you were delayed by certain thoughts and love for the world has allowed for your heart's desire to be what you are so eager to manifest, with your mighty powers. Yes it can come to be, and you ask yourself before you really there.

What's the difference, between trying to achieve something and really accomplishing it the way is meant to be, and knowing that you cannot have peace without it making sense and you are finally there? When you have walk the talk and there's nothing holding you down and you have reached the end permanently. That is what will give you that little feeling of satisfaction with the whole of life. To have traveled the way and never giving up until everything is here, all of it, and how you had pictured it would be.

Chapter Eleven

Breakthrough

It does occur after a very long time of working that you begin to understand what you doing. Is not like you were content of what has been happening, you just certainly become aware of everything that is going on around you. Your mind start clearing from all the frustrations and the confusion that you had been experiencing, and a lot of negative things start disappearing.

As it does happen that through the years you might have struggled with something very important, and for all that is worth it has lasted longer than expected. So long that you cannot pretend like it didn't have an effect on you.

We try to be very patient, only that some things are just unbearable. Regardless of how hard one tries to be discipline, it becomes difficult to overcome them that simply, and you find yourself pushed to the edge, until you feel like breaking.

Maybe so much is who we are and what we want to achieve, and the thing about ever going through a period of breakdown is that the way out is never there. Things can keep following you everywhere you are, whereas from the beginning it was just about discovering a purpose which will give your life meaning.

You will feel like blaming yourself for ever wanting more out of life or seeking for true love, and as far as you have traveled is hard to let go of that ambition, as you cannot find the way in the meantime. When things have gone wrong, we change our purpose, hoping to reach for something that could give us the satisfaction. Be able to arrive where we are meant to be human that have witnessed happiness, and have truly achieved joy in everything that we do.

Once you're lost it can be a battle to ever find meaning. If you have never fought for self-worthiness, this will be the first time you had to acknowledge a true spiritual battle.

Is what it becomes, as you struggle with yourself to see the way, no matter how big and broad the world might feel outside. It is within that you fighting the toughest battle which you must win, more like there's a wall that restrains you from reaching out to the whole of life. Whenever you send a signal it comes back to you with no good results. Even when you try to make contact you cannot be felt or received, everything has been shuttered by lack of understanding.

You cannot know everything at once, we learn so much as we go through with life, what you are currently is not the best that you can do. Underneath you're still capable of more potential which for now could be hard to reach to. In order to arrive at that place where you clearly understand what you doing, you must be dedicated to your course until you have a clear picture on how to do what you love, and that's how it must be. We prepare ourselves or what we know and when we feel like we have done our best to be understood we send it, or maybe go out there, which is where you want to be received or accepted.

For a very long time you're locked within and you cannot get out of that shell, to experience how it feels to live through your own understanding. So to break out of the self-imprisonment that you've created with your willingness to have greater achievements, you work hard and resemble courage.

Mostly it is here at the beginning where we go through this kind of difficulties which we find it hard to pass through, and become our true invention. You are tired of the old self, now you want something new, is not like you don't have enough or maybe you desperate for life, you seek for a way to be content with who you are.

You want to find where you belong, and what you worth, you stop thinking less about yourself. Now that the real world has challenged you, and apart from what you have known, there's something greater which you must discover about you. For so long you could have lived a lie, of assuming that you matter whereas you don't, you have been working in vain.

Now is time to experience the reality of your own truth, in actual fact you wish you can walk right through that glass of dreams that separates you from the life you wanted to live. We only hope that maybe the will was enough, to have had the eager to be part of everything, and that being the only thing you need to be the star you desire.

As for now you're locked down right at the very beginning of your life, holding on to something which could be your next identity, yet not ready for the world. It seems to be a part of ourselves where you cannot beg your way through. You work for everything that you want, and you understand that you can never be of that life, if you haven't brought your unique understanding.

Is what creates a room for you to matter, and you need to be good at what you do as without something that truly speaks volume of what you are, you no one, and you are not to be recognized, you earn your name.

It is likely that when we have identified a certain goal, is meant for everything that we desire. So you've had a rough start in love or maybe you have been lucky that from the beginning, or along the way you picked up someone who is exactly the way you wanted. They have been able to give you all that you needed, and that satisfies your life in a way that you don't seek for so much anymore. You are just where you need to be, or maybe you wanted a good relationship, and things never worked out as great as you've required them to.

For as long as you have lived you holding on to that goal, which you've had for the rest of your life, and it doesn't seem to come easily, as there's that part of not being exactly where you need to be. As we do breakdown in love, but in order to find the same true love, you're required to break out of it. Have quality lifestyle that will attract the same in everything.

As there's something that makes us realize that what we experiencing is a fall, is the relationships that we had which had been the best. They had so much to share and everything to live for, things were just so great and the way you wanted them to be.

Then at the end you want to comeback after you had separated with the one you could have loved truly, and regardless of what the world use to offer you. It is difficult to have that kind of life with another one, they are just not there anymore, and you can try to find a relationship to commit to.

Whereas there's none, and how can you be out in the open with someone who doesn't feel like you are the best thing that they have ever had, it doesn't work that way. For a communion to produce satisfaction it must have a strong bond from within, and for as long as we live we still long for that kind of commitment that we have had which was everything to live for.

Whether it was the first time or not you have had the best experience, and once your body feels that kind of bliss. It wants more of it every day, and we never go back in life, or maybe in love. We growing up moving forward and building value on what we have become, or passed through so far. Regardless of where we headed you need a good relationship, for you to be happier, and the sad thing is that you cannot have that with everyone who comes to be part of you every day. It only comes once in a while, the rest is a lie.

Feels irrelevant compared to what you need to be settled with everything or achieve about your life, that's where you felt the pain of lacking true love. It emerged from being ignored, knowing it was once there, and now you're unable to get that which you require to be happy, or you can begin something from the scratch. Though you might not know where is headed and how the end will be.

So much just feels good about what you becoming, and we never really know that this is true or decide from the beginning that this is what we want to be. It becomes an expression, you express how you feel about things, until you get used to it.

The part that manifests as true love is through commitment, you kept going deeper and deeper with it until you disappeared, and when there was not much left. You became the new formation which is everything to live for, and as people we have different interest and they could lead us to that place we truly seek to be in so many ways.

Though you could have undermined those efforts until you were left with that gift as the only way forward, or towards which you must live your life. Now you want nothing except for that way, and regardless of how relaxed we are about it. Comes that time where we must push it to the world, and if you don't possess that kind of determination you can never do it.

So it became like a maze, the only place where you're stuck, and without ever breaking through you cannot do it any more, you just require so much to make sense. For regardless of how you try to do it, at some point you need a little bit of push, so that it can work out the way it is supposed to.

Is this what you really want, is what you have done enough, do you need to give more or everything is fine the way you had been doing things? As something must be there that passes you to the other side of your life, and it hasn't been who you are as you know you cannot do it naturally.

It will need something more to happen, and to stretch your horizon just a little bit, is it not what brings the star in us out to life? You wouldn't shine if you didn't have that super strength that you need to apply in order to pass all the levels that are there.

We are not from that level, we work with our mind, body, and thoughts to achieve that kind of understanding. As we are not gifted in everything that we will want to be, some things that we want to bring to the world are hidden beneath the surface of our knowledge, and to reach for it you must push yourself.

We are not birthed with the perfect vision of how things must be done. So much is what you learn along the way, and it becomes a breakthrough as you didn't know anything about the world and what you doing. You learned every day, studied night and day until things began to make sense, is what you needed to understand about yourself. That we are born with enough knowledge just to get us from one place to another, and we study everything that we know, and even with studying we don't get things completely or everything correct.

Some things are just there for us to work on them on our own, so imagine this road, how challenging, lonely, and heart-breaking it has been. As it required more than you have inside, which we don't know if that's a divine spirit or not. Just that something was able to walk you through that path of life until you began understanding. As it doesn't happen every day that when you begin this life you will know or find the way to the end easily, is the will that one has that keeps on leading the way.

It all begins with an idea which you might not even be sure that will ever make sense, as you may not be certain of what you're capable of. You never really know if you are good at something or you just taking a risk, one day you could discover a way to do a certain thing, however that alone is not enough.

You strive to excel until you become the best that humanity has come to see, you think about what you are, how far you need to go, or how good you want to be. Yet for now you don't understand that much about the world and everything that you doing.

The goal becomes a way of love that you travel through to that place where you need to arrive at, and for a very long time you're not as good as you want the outcome to be. Your desire is just a wish you have which you want to explore, and until then, you are not sure of anything.

The ambition is bigger than what we are at the beginning, and when you want to carry it through, you fall and stumble that you can't even stand straight any more. As it is heavy and that is how we earn the strength and the experience of everything that we becoming.

You wish for something that you will love to be part of, and when time comes to make a decision about your life. Now you have a perfect plan that will allow you to live for so much that you value, and instead of setting a goal that will not mean much. You are aiming for everything that you worthy of, and when you get to achieve that at the end, it would have been a dream come true. You will have an opportunity to live happily ever after, and you are content as you've given yourself to an ambition you can manage to reach for.

Is not like right now you can do it beyond what so many are capable of doing things, so a need to be dedicated more is necessary. Which for now you don't know how, and it exists on the inside that you have the potential to do whatever you desire. As you have set the goal that you want to achieve with everything that you can produce as part of your understanding.

How can you push yourself beyond the limits, and overcome that mental block, that has your life standing on hold, and you cannot pass it when you want to. You have to grow into it, as it must develop through you so that it can come to existence.

The fact that you have it within you, and that being the reason why you decided to act upon it. We don't set our limits when we work for so much that we love about ourselves, you define the area of life where you feel competent.

As it happens all the time that there are just those things which is not who you are, and for you to be safe you choose exactly what you understand, as something that you can do to an acceptable level. When required acknowledge that you cannot be everything, you can only be what you desire, and be the best at it.

If you have figured what you love which communicates directly to your inner self, then there's nothing that you should be afraid of. Regardless of how you feel challenged at some point, you choose how far you want to make your mark, and after you have decided on that then the way is free.

As you get to set your perspective towards your horizon, on the contrary failing to focus your mind on that, cripples your understanding as you don't know how to channel your thoughts. The goal and the territory becomes the foundation by which you must follow through to reach where you going. We don't begin with a complete plan, we develop from the objective and the will we have inside.

After that we don't remember what we use to be, all we know now is what we have become, and something reaches perfection as you could have been working on it for a very long time, then you begin to understand it the way is meant to be, a breakthrough to complete understanding doesn't come easy. If you ever achieve it, becomes an encouragement that uplifts you, and begin to see everything clearly. It allows you to connect with the world that you want to communicate with, and creates a sort of a platform by which you get to be recognize.

It might not mean that you completely know everything, it could be a reflection of the fact that you now exist at a level where you understand yourself better. As you could have long lived in the dark, without a clue of what's happening out there, this way became the light to see through things which you might not have realized existed.

It means that so much will not remain hidden from you, and regardless of what you come across you will not stumble and fall apart. Even though you cannot explain how it happened, yet it became a way that one needs to hold on to.

Maybe you have been struggling with an idea to create something wonderful, and you don't know how. All you have is the picture and how it supposed to happen, and is hard to understand how to make it work for everyone to love it. We always face this kind of issues which we don't have the knowledge how to carefully create a certain invention to life, where you're understood correctly the way you intended. A concept that is received with pure understanding without having to say so much.

When you instantly send the message out there you're heard precisely how is meant to be, and without having to tell anyone what you mean, everybody realizes your goals.

A lot of what you use to be begins to lose meaning from that, when you certainly commit yourself to a goal which you trying by all means to get right. Your complete energy becomes focused on that, more like you are now separating yourself from everyone who is part of your life.

Whatever they had known about you has now become less significant, you're turning into something they have never expected of someone, and as much as they haven't known that about you. It feels as if you're neglecting them for your personal needs and well-being.

So much can become meaningless and what could now means the world to you, is the desire which you have chosen to devote your time to. It must come to existence regardless of what the cost could be, and at that point where you are willing to do everything to make it happen at the expense of all that you have known or understood about life. You have crossed over to the other side of manifestation.

So many times to pass from one level to another, we constantly need to make promises and bind ourselves with our goals as we go along the way. That is what we have given our lives to, despite the challenges we go through, and that strengthens you to pull what you love back to you without expecting how it became possible, since it was what you wanted.

The world cannot deny you what you want if you are willing to sacrifice whatever it may be for it to manifest. What you give is what you get out of anything, and just like that it has cost you so much love you had to share. Now you only have that goal as your main priority, and is what stand above the rest as a key to a full life and happiness.

So that which you strive to have at the expense of what you are, is what will come to be, and that is what we face every day or at a certain point in our lives. Is the passion we resemble that opens the door for our deepest desires, if you feel like holding on to what you were then you cannot have it the way it is. You empty your heart for your priorities to fill it, you need to fulfill the eager to have what you desire.

You make it your priority as it has become the only thing that is important to you, at some point we are faced with choosing what means everything to us. So when true love as well becomes what you want at a given period in your life, is what you will get, as you have resembled faith to have it.

Until then it can wait, as there are more important things that you need to be dealing with, and is not like you don't feel the sacrifices that you making, it is painful. Though you only made time for what you eagerly seek to manifest, if you don't give love to something then it cannot force itself on you, only what we want comes to be.

For someone who has created priorities, you will experience your joy coming to life. So you understand that being the best is there in you, and exactly where is supposed to be. Only needing you to push yourself a little harder than usual, and that's where the magic is, we have it within us, somehow it must be what you want to see, and you don't blink. You put it first and above everything, and for what is worth to all that we have left behind we no longer go back, we begin to identify this as the new beginning of the future that we have.

Refuse to ever go back to that person that you were, and to those places that you use to visit, we have so much that we were living for. Which is what we walked away from, and now a lot that we want is in the future, and regardless of how difficult it could be to break through that wall, with determination to move forward.

You have the strength and the most unbelievable will to pass so much that there is, and everything is what you will get, and not in the past you have lived in, where you headed. So instead of taking one thing at a time, have a goal that embodies all that you need.

Treasure what you want more than anything, which is the goal that you seek to achieve, and put it first, and right where it must be and move through it. So that you can experience change and a life which is no longer what it used to be, though somewhere you will start from the scratch.

Love you have as well in your heart, and you know that it is the most important thing that will complement everything that will come to exist. As for now it can wait, is not like it doesn't matter, the thing is that it will come to be of importance after everything has fallen into place.

When you have arrive at your destination of hope, everything will make sense. As for now you holding on to this ambition that you have, which is everything to live for, and if you look away a lot will come to pass. So you see the part where all that you need depends on you, and though you want it altogether, the love, and life, besides being the star you appreciate so much. So put it right where it must be, let this goal that you have in your heart and in so many ways be what you strive for, and letting it be the worth you continue to embrace.

Breakthrough all that you have ever known, as a lot that we are becomes the walls that are imprisoning us and refusing to see a change in what we are. Even love can stand in the way of so much that you need, the life that you live on a daily basis can refuse for you to become something else. As we became accustomed to those ways we had been on for the rest of our lives.

So much that we have been can turn to be like a curse, even so, you are the one meant to choose what you want to be, and how far you are willing to go with the journey you have begun. If you are to break boundaries then let the worth decide the way, and what is more valuable?

So you let the ultimate goal be the driver, which is what matters the most and you know that traveling through this path will be the solution. That will be what achieves all that you desire, or you can let anything be what leads the way. Only that it doesn't care about what you truly want, so what is it that you really need, you make your own choice.

You can let love drive you forward and through it you break into every wall that there is, and anything which exist, or you can let the goal you have for everything be the main objective. That you're prepared to slave for and then it will be what creates sense, at the end.

It will be what life in you became, and through it you can achieve all that you need, so decide which one is better for now, relationships or the goal to stand out and be the best. As both might be very strong, or maybe you take them together, and see through them, so you let the love lead you towards everything there is.

Meaning that whatever you're committed to is enough the way it is, or if you feel that the ambition alone is sufficient to lead your life moving towards your greatest desire, and be what gives you your worth. You take it, so what becomes the way?

If you already have true love, you let it drive you toward your greatest desire, knowing that the goal exist in you as well. You acknowledge that you can't let love down, or someone who has loved you beyond everything be disappointed as you have a dream and a vision that you want to bring to light.

That affectionate will be what carry you through everything, and from it a different world will come to exist. So if loneliness has torn your heart into pieces, don't find yourself looking for something which isn't there. You just keep on traveling the way you started, and not that love isn't important.

It is essential, and it will be the best to live for, as for now you need your whole life. To make that dream come true, and bring that vision into reality, regardless of how difficult it could be. You let it be the priority that you have in your heart, and it will manifest all that you are, the love, and the perfect life that you've always wanted will be worthy of you. It was here at the end where everything became possible, it didn't matter how difficult it was, and through that faith in what you are everything was able to come alive.

Chapter Twelve

Love Again

You cannot be imprisoned in your own way of thinking, something must become of you. The most painful part of everything is after you've lost someone and you need another chance to find true love. You want a way back to that special person's loving arms, it doesn't have to be the same individual. Losing a relationship to being focused happens very often, as commitments needs attention, and it is likely to come back and catch up with you as we at times let go without a reason. You no longer feel any purpose to be doing it, why?

You don't know why, it could be that everything has got a point where it is no longer important compared to how you feel things should be happening, and you're convinced that if I can ever break through this. Maybe I will fall in love with the right person at the other end, and justifies the kind of dedication we give to all that we have become. How would you be sure of what awaits on the other side of life, if you have never given all that you are to something that you want to see?

To love is our only gift, if you have ever given yourself to a worthy cause, is true love that will justify the life that you've been dedicated to. The thing is that we devote so much of who we are if we want to witness success. We become so weak and remain with nothing to live for, and if you have value you will know as you can never give up on a true communion forever. It will be there for you to understand that whenever you're ready to be human again, you must submit to it, with all your heart.

So much dies out of a human being in the quest to find your essence, and is not supposed to be like that, somehow it feels so right to have gone through such a pain of love. As hard as relationships can be to maintain, we allow it to pass a little bit, so that true love can be what we settle for at the end. I have never known why the need to give up.

We force things at times, knowing it isn't who we are, and we can try to say we are just trying to make it happen as far as life is moving on in the meantime, and you can be embarrassed by situations that you can go through. When love is real, and someone is in it as they're willing to commit to you all the way. Become very blessed and able to stretch the horizon to create happiness, in all areas of your life.

You find yourselves dragging each other down by choosing to be in love when you not ready to settle. "At some point I knew that I was there, I had tried to be strong for relationships to pass, still, you cannot overlook everything, and so much has a hold on us. It could be in any occasion, the fact that you are a human being and you do take your chances on situations, makes you feel bad about yourself," and yes it is true. It feels wrong as if someone is there to rob you of the only life that you have.

How can you let something which isn't true take away the only thing that you've ever valued, and settle for a part of your life which isn't love. If true love isn't there, you have nothing to give to each other, and you cannot sacrifice anything about who you are. To try and please someone else while you need to give to yourself as well. Is the beauty that we hold inside, what we eager to see before the wonder of this world?

It feels like so many can relate to the love we have for something to become a reality. And they can't, it becomes your battle of fighting for what you believe in. Which only exist in your world, and is what you're prepared to see come to existence. If you try hard at some point you can settle for a part of life which is very low about someone, and it can happen when you force things.

That you can fall deeper than you can ever pull yourself out, to a level so irrelevant about true love or commitment. So if you wait for the right time you can find exactly what you deserve, which is true communion.

"Standing there I wondered when it came to love if I should at some point tell my own story, of how I felt things that made me become this person that I am, how complicated a simple thing became difficult to understand."

I had given myself to a cause which I was very passionate about, that led to my breakthrough and became my bigger perspective on life. Somewhere along the way it felt like the world around me didn't understand what I have become. As it was something beautiful, and unexpected of someone, and the time in which I had hoped for things to make sense became a lifetime, as there was no support. Everything turned against the person that I am, and now I needed to fight hard to be a normal human being again, and I didn't like how I became a victim of my own creativity.

I had tried to put up a good fight however sooner or later, it began to show that there was something wrong inside, and the kind of treatment that you get from everyone. You can try to overlook so much and keep on living. Still, the fact that when you down like that there's nothing that you can offer to someone became the life I had to accept as the only way I lived on a daily basis.

You can try to accept yourself unlike to be depressed all the time, given the fact that you don't need to take it out on human beings, and is it really necessary to act negatively? For you cannot be completely isolated, as you are being compelled to, you make means to get along with as many people as you can. Hoping that the future will be better, and to be pushed out of life like that, you feel completely powerless to be human again so easy, and you can't give yourself to anyone, or trust your heart with someone.

Not now, things don't make any sense in the meantime, yes you couldn't be completely right about everything that is true. You never know where you headed or what to expect, even though your love for so much has died. You try to be honest about that virtue which you value more than all that exist, and that's what at the end justifies the need for the eager we feel on the inside.

Regardless of what could have changed or went wrong, you meant well, and had no intentions to harm. It was true love that led to this direction of life, and without it you cannot be at peace.

You can try to find something to hold on to, and it would make a lot of sense to do that, if anything has turned against you. As you feel the strain for that kind of touch you have lost with life, and you do die somewhere deep within, as everything was eventually based on that love you had for the world. When you have given your utter faith to a certain aspect of understanding, when that thing collapses, your whole belief disappears with it.

When your world has died and there's nothing to hang on to, you try to be part of existence, and it doesn't make any sense. You become too broken and a pain to be around people, and maybe we try hard to hold on to so much, only that if we can let go, we could find life very easy to live. Holding on to so much in the present becomes a crime you committing as is not who you are.

When denied what you want, you're refused to love, so much can go wrong and relationships can suffer from that, as it is an outside influence. A lot can come into play just to destruct you to ever be normal in that area, and you feel subjected so bad to carry through your objectives. You can pass that as well, it can be a lesson to learn for the rest of your existence.

The need to give up so much in the present and make a room for your heart's desire cannot be overlooked. As it is at times the best way in which one can do things, and you not abandoning life or rather love. If you have faith and belief in what you doing you cannot fail to carry your ambitions to existence. Especially if you have convinced yourself of the reality that you want to see, you cannot stumble and fall.

Though trying to accommodate so much can weigh you down so bad, and not to ignore the fact that you had everything to live for, and you had to let go. As you needed to make way for that deep desire, and one thing that needs to be looked at carefully, is that whether one loves or not; once your normal routines are compromised relationships cannot be quality, something has got to show for it.

Deep within you know that quality love exists somewhere, and that's what you want to live for, and it has been everything you wanted to be part of. True love overflowing with abundance that you cannot overlook it for anything, and you can keep holding on to this present situation. Yet it isn't what will give you all you need, or what you truly desire to be happy. A worthwhile relationship will once again be possible through your understanding, and without cheating yourself.

You love that it would be everything to live for at the end, regardless of how you have to travel there, you have faith that if you ever get things right the world has saved that for you. All this giving yourself to anything along the way is nothing except trying to fight a war that you have already lost long ago. Love does exist which isn't settling for less than what you are, true love that respects all that you've become.

You could let the present decide your life just that abandoning everything now to find meaning in the future is the right thing to do. Is what seems to be the place where we are better people at committing ourselves. If you have fail in the meantime, regardless of what could have led to your disappointment. You could need to forget about today and look at the world ahead and hope for something meaningful.

Maybe we never have the discipline for this kind of life that we desire, if you have self-control and worthiness you understand how to value what you aiming for. This holding on to what cannot give you what you want is not conducting yourself properly. Proper behaviour is letting go, valuing your defined goals to love which is what you want to be happy about.

The thing that becomes weak about holding on to something unworthy, is that it has a way of dragging you down, and slow your progress until you become so hopeless to see the way. You find yourself worn off on everything and to all that matters, not that we refuse to love, there's just no reason and motivation enough for one to stick around, and you can get there. You just need to get up and never look back, feel yourself leaving everything behind to find true love.

If you ever compromise love, you would have jeopardize all you desire to be a happy person. Bear your pain, not to suffocate whoever comes in your life, and it can be like that when you lack discipline, and so much could happen as if is worthy. And is not, as much as there won't be any justification for the character you lack motivation to resemble in conducting yourself.

It is necessary, and it will always be one of those things which you mustn't refuse to be strong about. Be content of the world you live in, and be courageous if you still have the will to achieve greatness.

You know that to let go can never be that easy or make any sense, and belonging, where do you belong? Are you part of the weakness called your past, or are you about the future which is your full life. Is that simple, you just stand there and declare your intentions to yourself, you decide now. As you can work night and day without ever being weary, thinking that it is creating somewhere, whereas is not. Until you're fully sure of your motive, you working for nothing, all that you doing doesn't amount to anything that is real about love.

Can you let your love be stolen from you, the dream that you fully aware is everything to live for, disappearing before your own eyes? We decide in so much about ourselves, is what you intending that becomes the life you live. You might not know all there is about the world, but you can be sure of how to proceed within that channel which has now become available through the will you have inside.

Which is supportive of your future, and is there to be a pillar of strength in our day of need, or to our routines. So now when you refuse to be part of it, everybody looks at you as if you don't have a place in their lives. Since you've lost your purpose, which could have brought a lot of good to you.

How far do we know about our own world, for to understand something at times feels so wrong? As our knowledge has a limited capacity, and you cannot force things to happen beyond being the person that you are. Is that level of knowing that controls everything that comes into our lives, and in most instances it must be enough, and where you draw the line.

That no matter how far you travel there's just those boundaries that you have drawn for yourself, and make sure is your deepest desire that you need, and which you after, and is not to live for nothing. Is to be a human being for that part that you love about life.

Whatever you know can be everything, and love if you allow it to. You decide for your own good, and look away from everything that you know doesn't serve your interest, and that transcending level of your understanding. Life produces what we worth, is where we find that special person who not only crowns our efforts, it is love where is true. Be faithful, knowing that kind of commitment can be freed within us, if we are where we must be.

There is part of our lives that you know is not free inside, as you haven't achieved your goals. You can wonder around with it trying to know if you will ever be happy, and we pretend like it doesn't exist, and it does. There is a platform for everything that we are, and that's where we're always happy to find whatever we need. Not below your standard, that's settling for something you not, exactly what you worth.

When do we actually settle for who we are, knowing that this deserve our true love and attention, and nothing can ever question that about you. When so much has been taken away from you, and you are only left with the will to drive you forward. You might need to travel with caution, as so much can come and destruct you, if you are not focused on the way like you should. Know the goal, love it and fix your eyes on it, for it has become your only way to have again.

Do you regret the life you were meant to live, and you feel so denied the power to be human easily that you can wonder at that opportunity over and again? It depends on the drive and determination that one has, if you truly are determined you cannot regret what you need to be even when things don't go well sometimes.

It could be that if you not fully prepared you might have second thoughts, and dwelling in your past. So much that we were meant to be which is for us and everyone, is what we refuse about ourselves, and take a new journey which is about you alone, and everybody gets to matter at the end.

What are you refusing to accept about yourself, knowing is what stands out about you. Is what you have chosen enough for all that you need? Yes it might be everything that one requires. "When the world wasn't here and everything around was heart-breaking, I chose myself.

I decided on being something which is a goal for me, and that was able to pick me up, and instead of being broken down to pieces by my present situation. I felt very courageous to do a lot of good, and to know that this will be the life I now live as my ultimate objective, and my way to happiness which I'm fully prepared to embrace."

When there's nothing to hold you up, and everything is just heart breaking with no one to care for you and let alone look after. How would you have made it, or survive that period? You can accept being alone when you understand the reason why. When you don't know the significant of it, you made your way to become a human being again, and now you have been living through that. How can you betray your whole life and the only thing that recreated your purpose, and when you're unfaithful to the goal, then there's no future?

The goal is meant for us to become strong individuals, that understand how to be physically and fully focused. Now when something comes along before you reach your destiny, you know very well and see what it is, only that is not how you pictured your life at the end. You realize that beauty has been stolen out of it, to be who we are is to hold on to the wonder of life, and the objective that made you travel this way.

The thief; remember that whatever has stolen your life from the beginning will always be after everything that you value, and nothing ever goes back to what it was. If something has decided to take from you, it will forever follow everything that you worth. Even when is no longer necessary, and we all can go through such stages in our lives.

Now if you've never lost anything to this world you can fail to see the part where we find ourselves stuck, and is how things will turn out. Even when you reach the end, don't hope for any luck of happiness, unless you're within your creation. Is then that you're not set up, and you know situations are real.

The rest of what we go through is man-made situations, where you're left with self-pity for which if you knew how to be someone useful to their desires, and what you've dedicated your life to. You would've known how to avoid, if you ever look away from the goal and what it can produce as part of your understanding. You will truly witness being a failure, don't fail yourself to find true love again, even though we are always tempted to be involved in things that don't deserve our attention.

Whatever we find unworthy is the opposite of what is life, don't settle for something which you aware completely doesn't represent you. It mustn't be on someone's terms, let it be on your own will, that's when it will make sense, or create meaning. The way will treat you to the end of everything that you know, and you might think is about you, and what you aiming for. Of which is not, the enemy is always that big, and can come for all that you are.

You may assume that is with respect to you and the situation that you facing, and is not, is about you not achieving what you truly desire. Remember that whatever can aim at your life, can be aiming higher than you ever expected, and the best thing to do could be to keep your focus. You can only set your passion free by setting a goal which cycles all your needs, and you keep on going until you find yourself within that arena of your ambitions where you're meant to find happiness.

Where your goals are, is meant for you to see yourself perfectly, living your life normally. Is not that today doesn't matter, it is important, it might be that if it was not what you had set for you so much could be wrong in a way that you can keep fixing things or maybe it might never work. So much is that you can find things, only that is not what you intended, and settling for something so small will be a waste of all your time, at the end.

We are not randomly selected by situations, you get to choose what to become. You can be influenced badly by the world or people without understanding how it came to be possible. Yet be happy that along the way you became useful to your own creativity, unlike having your thoughts rejected for the rest of your life, we have so much to live for and to admire about our lives. Still, make sure is what you truly love or desire about yourself, don't get caught up in things that will not offer you something worthy for the person that you are.

The problem is that is not something that you can build your hopes on, you have to prepare yourself for better tomorrow, knowing that you cannot rely on luck. It feels like we fortunate, and that's not building a stable solution, a good reliable future is built on capabilities. You capitalize on what you know that you are best at, and you put your whole trust and beliefs on it, what if along the way things don't happen as you have hoped.

You had relied on chances favoring you, while you needed a good strategy, which becomes your concrete foundation, and is meant to give you what you want. Plans don't fail or disappoint, only hopes can disappear and defy the reality by which you were to rely on. We have so much to live for through a life that is well planned, and so little to build our lives on and being confident that success will come through luck.

Everything feels like a set-up, knowing that the world will never offer you anything to rejoice about. Even when it seems like you're been given something, It is still taking, and it will forever be consuming you. At some point you have to understand that you must give back to yourself, you are the only one who truly understand who you are, and what you need. You will ask why me, and that could be the exact point in your life where you must pose that question, and the answers could lie deep within you.

Is nothing except for that path which you have chosen or what you have become so far. Not caring what you could be looking for, and how you have done it, even if it means that you must understand so much. As that could be where the force that fights you comes from, how did it all began, where is it emerging from, and when does it end? It could have emerged from you seeking your own way or understanding and ended up influencing everything that you are, and it ends with you being satisfied, with achieving your goals.

We don't really know what we're meant for, we could be destined for so much, and if you can follow through that ambition. You might find something worthy of the love you have inside, and at times when looking at the outside world. You wonder how does one end up giving themselves to a part of life which is not who they are, and you can see what it has turned them into.

It has done them so bad that it doesn't feel like it will ever be all right, it has ruined their lives somewhere so deep that sorrow lingers in their soul, and that should be a lesson enough for you to be fond of who you are.

If you make a bad choice about your life or the future you will forever suffer that setback, and you can pretend like you will understand and it will never make sense. What has passed of you was that chance, and so much that follows ahead is just meant to ruin your opportunity for success. You can fight countless battles to be content of who you are, and all you had to be aware of was always there from the beginning of time.

Hate how you misunderstand things, and work to create your own space where you will discover so much about your world, what you will come to understand. Is that to know is not enough, and the hard part will be not only knowing but becoming part of it yourself, as you cannot stand there and watch for the rest of your life. Though you coming through your own direction, you still need to make everything work beautifully and manifest your inner thoughts, cast the fear and be so much.

If you could only give yourself completely to something without a doubt, you don't know what could be the next best thing to follow. When a gift has been given to you, be happy and be more through it, just don't keep quiet, rejoice so much and be someone not only complaining about situations being bad.

Let it be that when good has happened, you are able to show that you do understand what has become a reality, as small as the world could feel when you're talented. It can have that sense of hatred beyond what you can handle, and you can only wish you had been able to find a different approach, so celebrate when you have a talent to interact with everyone.

All this which happened over the years has stolen nothing except for true love within you, where it used to be everything to live for, on the face of this beautiful world. Remember what you're born for, you could be meant for so much and you can never find that if you haven't risked anything and dedicate yourself completely to it, and if something was standing before you? What would you do about it, knowing that it wouldn't go away when you want it to, and you don't know when it will leave your life?

Would you succumb, being fully aware it isn't you who leads an objective like that. You have chosen a special purpose which will give you everything including true communion, and remember that true love is always aimed at by everyone else. As is one of the main ingredients to a fullness of life, and with love filled in your heart, so much can aim at you.

Knowing that you can never know who you were, and you have escaped a lot which isn't you to find your passion, so refuse to give in. Walk straight to the end of your understanding, hoping that it will be exactly what you want, and it can be possible if you hold on to your dreams.

As tired as you may be learn to keep going, as to give up is not meant for us. We are destined for true love, and as you pass that little obstacle which had been standing in your way. You are getting closer, so keep traveling ahead, for the best is still coming, as it has been what you wanted and don't go back without ever finding it.

Is there and waiting for you to live through, all this challenges that comes in your life don't come alone. They bring with them temptations, and you will be tempted until you don't know what to do, and don't be afraid of the stranger that you are to the whole of existence. Allow yourself to grow and become something new.

Let go of the person you no longer are in the world, and admire this beautiful being that you're becoming. True love that is worth your life is knocking in your heart, open up for it has given in and without a doubt it will be for you to offer yourself to it.

As it is worthy of so much, and don't avoid it when time comes as you worry that you not meant for it, is made for all that you are. The most exciting part is that you don't have to wonder how to love that person who you completely destined for each other, a relationship like that comes with everything.

I know true love has so much to do with being happy, and if that relationship you have doesn't produce that kind of feeling then you're not in love. It must be coming to create an everlasting happiness and you must both achieve it a way that is meant to be. A true communion when is how it must be, It is just there to make you a very good person, carry it to the end and agree within your heart that a gift like that is for you to treasure forever.

Chapter Thirteen

I Serve the World

After passing all these ups and downs in our act of creativity, as well as the struggles of love, your real life has begun, and for some time you don't know what to do. You lack confidence in yourself, though you've created a certain concept, through hard work and patience the entire world loves it.

We are always influenced by different things which become the shape of our reality, and that is how we begin to understand everything around us. Though is not something that you can be able to share with someone, except that you are falling for the whole of existence, and you saw where you could fit in appropriately.

It could have been that we all can settle for what we have where we are, and some find it very acceptable to live life like that, they're never keen on understanding what the world can offer them. They opened their hearts and be satisfied with so much including their simple less sophisticated lifestyles.

As different as we can be they have accepted themselves the way they are, and regardless of that language which the whole world speaks. They have chosen to make peace with who they are, though there is that global standard which everybody is supposed to meet, they have chosen to create their own level.

Unlike focusing on the environment around you, globally there is so much that you need to understand about people, and it might seem like a difficult thing to achieve. Of which is not that hard, when you have discovered a purpose that is true to yourself.

Regardless of how advanced certain cultures could be, there are things that are common about us people, which is what we are, what we feel, and that is the only thing real about everyone. The fact that the world is adorable and our requirements to move from one place to another, creates that sense of humanity's need for each other.

We don't just get lost, sometimes we lose ourselves spiritually and you need a friend from the other side to show you the way, and what you should have done which could have been the best solution in any or that given situation. That is regardless of how much one has, and that's how we relate to each other's conditions, and how to satisfy that need we have for life or love, to derive satisfaction from this world. So much affect us in the same way, you just have to be upfront about it, and find a space to share or maybe someone can associate to that.

That's what we usually do, we share the common difficulties we face on a daily basis. Which is the most exciting thing to understand about someone's life, the experiences we have had over the years, which are truly transformation. As we cannot encounter the same problems, when you see something that you love or relate to.

You are likely to associate that character with you, and you feel so strong about it as if it should be you, or is how you would've behaved or handle a certain situation. We don't only do this to entertain, we engage in it to inspire everyone who has the will inside.

As so many when faced with any situation which could be a challenge or the eager to have. Feel like is impossible and it cannot be done, and you who has witnessed success are there to show that if I can do it, so can you. Is nothing that I am which you not, I only had myself, and is not like circumstances are any different.

You as well have the same capabilities, is not about what you have that makes it all possible, is the will we have. Which is everything that you need to create a platform for communication, we don't have to do the same thing. We can engage in whatever we find necessary, which you know that through this path I will get as far as my world permits.

So you not imitating anyone you saw, you trying to reach for the stars through a path which you discovered in yourself. You know that this is what I'm good at, and people will love me for it, once you get a way to interact with the world. The next thing that you need to strive for is to make sure that you do it well and better than so many out there, and if it requires for you to work hard night and day, then do it.

Since it is the thing or rather the secret, you never know what someone has done for them to get there. You just witnessed the results of their work, and regardless of how they smile, it was there, people did work hard.

So you mustn't only have the will, also try to have the courage to get to that level which will say so much about you. At some point you see that being the best comes with the challenge, so you work for it, and it doesn't matter where you come from. You can be heard clearly or be understood, regardless of how the world is evolving. There are just those things which is what we must continue to teach each other about, which are the most important in any situation.

Value the will to make a change and continue to give love wherever is needed, preserve life and educate. The world needs that much from us, we teach other people about values and virtues which are the most important to show in any situation. You can get far with just the eager to do good and well to others, and do not only look at yourself as the center of attention, other human beings exist out there. With so much to tell regarding our lives that you will come to like and understand their point of views, and the difference they resemble.

So have your own values which are things that you hold dearly, and you know is just who you are, since as people we can never be the same. We have so much that differs within us, so that becomes your frame of reference, is what we know about you. Is how you are good and best in getting people to see that side of themselves.

Find the language which everyone will come to understand, and don't overlook something thinking that things do lose value. They don't, they will always mean what they did from the beginning of time, and let that be what you focused on so that you are understood clearly.

Respect the language which is used to interact with one another, and is there as it is the core of life. So once in a while after one has find themselves in a situation for which you have a skill for, or maybe you actually felt the pain they feel. It should be time to let everyone know what your suggestions on certain issues are. We all have a need to love, and that should be what we always focus on, as it is something that is timeless and touches us somewhere so deep.

Though we exist in different times, we can live each other behind as we dwell in various periods, some are living in a very advanced world. Still, that essence of life is what we need every day, through the many ways that are there to communicate our needs for true love.

The true reality about love never stop to exist, so do not just seek to be part of the world. Strive to understand it, its languages, and difficulties that we encounter every day. You could be anyone, yet pain has never left our lives and that's very important to acknowledge about what we are.

We share in each other's happiest and saddest moments, and you shouldn't engage in it as maybe you want to please someone. It should be what you are, what you truly desire, at whatever stage of life you could be, so much does catch up with us, and you might need someone to help you pass through that.

We share our true experiences of what we have come to understand so far, learning to love someone while loving the whole world. Going through the pain still holding on to your deepest self, as you cannot change anything about you. Whether is sad or deeply hurting, you have seen what you are, and you wouldn't give up what you've become. So much could have been difficult however we work on it until it gets easier, by continuously engaging in it, if you deem it being possible then you hold on with faith.

There are those who have never understood anything around them, all they see when they open their eyes is the world at large, and how they can become part of it. As it is you who decide for yourself what you want your life to be about, you wanted to live for so much, and carry the strength that can endure throughout the entire universe. You could have been weary along the way, and you never changed. You lived for the outcome and that gave you the energy to hold on tight to everything as it meant a lot to you.

Is not bragging about a life you only wish you can live, is giving yourself to living it, showing the character that you're required to resemble. As that's what it takes to deal with different types of people, and we don't just use that kind of understanding to please someone or ourselves.

They shape us to become the kind of individuals that we need to be, we were born in an ordinary world and not meant for so much. Through these virtues we became unique individuals with quality traits to share with everyone we meet or come across, as you need to be motivated for this kind of life.

Going out to the world human beings are made by different experiences, and if you didn't bring your toughest self, you can fall down thinking that people are bad while they're not. They are made by unique situations, and you didn't come prepared, so when it needs you to have patience, resemble it, and if it requires for you to have faith, remain true.

Have that quality it takes for an individual to be the best, as you do understand when looking at so many that they are at their most competitive level. So don't assume they had it any easier, they could be interacting with you through their strongest characters.

At times situations treat us to see how well prepared we are for the kind of people that we want to become, as human beings have bonds, and so much can hold you back. If you are ready for the life that you want to live, you train your mind so that you can walk right through any complex condition.

As you can come across circumstances that are very surprising without a clue on what has pushed you to that breaking point. While is what you have seen, you have witness a shocking world that is so challenging. As this are humans and they have different cultures and personalities, and we are required to know a lot about all that they are.

There's something that you need to understand, as there's that level of life where we meet, and exchange who we are as the world. Is a medium of the love we have for everything, so when that time comes to share who you are, make sure is quality you resemble to the whole of humanity. Though we never know as much as there is about ourselves as people, we just hoping that we learn enough that is required of one. So you adjust yourself to the requirements of the idea we seek to embrace.

With different people and their cultures you might need to come with a well-defined objective that stands out about your level of understanding. As you know this are human beings, and are made exactly by the same thing that has created your passion for life, and is what you can easily see on someone, though you refuse to believe it.

So when you going out there, prepare for everything that becomes the main theme that you want everyone to understand about your creativity. That is how we get to share our selves, and interact with each other, and you are there to serve that as a purpose.

So fulfill the objective which the world expect from you as an individual, who has given themselves to something that they love, and we continue to play our roles which are required from us. So ask yourself, what does the world seek from you as a person, what is your part in all of these, it doesn't matter what it could be?

If it forms the greatest characteristics of life then use that to communicate with other human beings. As they expect that from you, and to do what you have promised, so deliver on that which is expected greatly of you.

Beside what you coming out here to do, we serve a special purpose in people's lives. If you do exactly what you capable of, then you have arrived at that level where everyone actually gets to like you for what you know how to be. As regardless of being accepted to be part of the world, there's being loved, and to be that individual who inspires so many, that a lot feels so important whenever they interact with you. As you actually understand who they are and what they're going through, and that enable them to relate to your life easily, and that's one thing hard to find in a person.

No matter how advanced we are, that remain the only place where you must strive to arrive at, understand people's needs especially something which you know they need every day. You bring that experience of life, you have to be content of how to resemble caring, and it doesn't have to be specifically common with everyone.

It just have to be true about you, what kind of a world have you seen so far, and what has it done to you, or what is your understanding about love or maybe true love. What is the difference between now and then, going through it all and coming out as the person that you are.

What made you endure, when things were not going well what kept you strong, as it is the kind of message that we trying to get across from one person to another. Someone wants to know how it happened, and how were you able to handle the pressure. "Am I not being side-lined, since maybe I don't belong?"

We need that warmth of belonging somewhere, you are here to show caring.

People want an individual who is prepared to spread the gospel of hope, and to carry these virtues as a human being coming to the world is not easy. You feel a force that pushes you backward and you're required to thrust ahead, like we are not meant to be this kind of human beings who at the end we suppose to become.

We're not always conscious of what we do and how we have done it. You only become sure and aware when you begin to create the kind of person who is the perfect version of the life you need to live. How all that we did has become a little darkness in us, and let alone that you didn't have it in you. So you fight to push that out, until you connect to the new individual that is who you meant to be. As we've never known that we are destined for greatness, we would have prepared ourselves from the beginning.

You want to be the center of attention, but you understand that the world doesn't rotate around you. Is not that human beings cannot like you the way you are, they can love so much about you. So you don't have to change a thing about yourself, and we can't go back to the past where everyone seemed to be concerned with very important things in our lives such as true love.

Given that those people can never come back to continue in the journey they have begun. Only that we can take over and be the ones that preserve the virtues of our beautiful planet, at the end is us who live in it.

That should be the main issue we're concerned about, trying to save our universe, not the world that has come to pass. You become concern about what you see, what affects everyone on a daily basis. After all is in this present moment where we matter and where is important to be said, everything that we are is right now, and we help in explaining the age that we live in.

As there are a lot of people accelerating with time, doing good and bad things, and we equip ourselves to be the teachers of that. Is what we have been preparing for, you get to be the expert of the life being lived.

We don't exist as the only people who are here to teach about life. Although some teachings are felt irrelevant as they focus on things which are not what creates, and though is trying to bridge the gap between realities and fantasy. You cannot have everyone live in that imaginary world, human beings are concern about what's real. What makes or affect them, and that seems to be unnecessary.

As some prefer to understand their essence, and how their decisions can affect the future as it should have been, and yes we don't know everything there is about the universe. Somewhere deep within we want to be taught about virtues and how to preserve them.

That's where we serve something very vital to the world, trying to have our daily lives travel normal with a good pace while focused on what matters, and that shouldn't be stolen away from us. People mustn't be happy or live well at the expense of others, for something is who we are and we cannot exist without that part which is our share of life.

As it does happen that if the truth is not being told, there are things which are creating to steal that tender out of humanity. Regardless of that we still want things the way they are, we need to mature on issues like love. We don't want to be rushed into parts of creation which doesn't make up for our deepest self.

We don't wish to be subjected when it comes to how we perceive things should be done, or be put under pressure by entities which are not created with care for humanity. We want to learn how to create value, and have the right to choose what we really love about life. We wanted to fulfill goals, and find those capabilities that we have inside.

If needs be we require to discover more about ourselves, or even find the Divine creation of our lives. "Is what we desire and that ought to come to reality." So there's nothing that must steal away the tender from anyone, we still feel like part of the world has to remain the way it is.

That's the purpose we continue to encourage, as the thief is coming for all that matters out here, and if we allow it to be taken away from us. Then we will remain with nothing to live for, we need those people who are here to let us know it is possible. If you can bring it, to everyone's attention, after working hard on it.

Knowing that you didn't fake anything about the love, the life, and everything which is the main ingredient to quality, and you brought that true nature of caring and devotion. As we do feel that the world has advanced, still, somewhere deep within we remain longing for the reality of creation.

Someone can always tell whether you're true or not, there's that thing which we know is always real about people and you can feel it, if this person is telling the truth or lying. So we remain honest not only to ourselves, to the world at large, as it is what everyone wants to know about themselves. It doesn't change, it continues being the same about human beings, it doesn't matter who and where you come from. When all has faded away that's what we keep inside, as the theme of life, and you can never have it any easier.

It all comes through hard work and dedication, is not just the will which is enough, and needed to get you there. Is everything that you are on a daily basis, being prepared to share part of yourself with human beings. We do things until we believe it is the only thing that we are meant for, you don't look at what everybody is doing. You focus on your goals, there has to be something you embrace about life. You have to believe that people will find an angle to relate to what you are, as you gave your love for it to be true.

So ask yourself whether you really understand what it means or have what it takes, to share your knowledge with the world. Life is an ancient history, even so, there's something that we kept about that part of ourselves to this day we live in. As we value that thing about who we are, so much is what you understood from the beginning. You just never knew what it meant, to the time you had to be the one who embodied that truth, and you carry it until it becomes the virtues that you practice every day.

The world will accept that about you and you will pass it to the next person who seeks to understand who they are, and where they belong. A lot are so curious about things, they want to create themselves with that knowledge, and you help them achieve that.

You wanted a purpose to serve and that should be enough for what you exchange with everyone. So many need to find that connection with all of life in order to fix those mistakes that they have committed. Which are now becoming in their lives, and they want to cast that out of their essence.

Someone could have come to realize that part of their lives as they have some precious possession to value and they want to keep it. So much can drive us too far and there's no need to destroy anything about ourselves, when you feel so pushed to the end of your life, and feeling the need to hang on to something.

Then hold on to love, it does have true worth for everything that we are, we don't want to be distracted all over our entire understanding. As you don't know what can aim at you, but you understand that some things can pass with you.

We need to know what we part of and what isn't for us to understand, and don't deny yourself the truth. It does exist, and you can come to realize what we are after a very long time of being lost. As we do lose our way, everything is meant to drive us to that point where we stray away from our purpose.

Somehow it is disappointing as we don't want to be the product of that sad life which we could have witnessed. We desire good to come to our lives, and we truly don't require to be subjected to never finding happiness. We believe that it does exist at the end when you have shown courage that you become of great value.

You know where you going, then find a way to get there, value this human being that you are, as that's what matters about our lives. To achieve that true worth, and we need to break through these walls that exist with everyone and be understood by the whole of existence, and that's how we are. People living to find a way to the other side of all that we doing, and be loved for everything that we have become. You want to be accepted by the other for all that you are, and this is regardless of what the world has changed to.

Is the goal that we have set for ourselves and it doesn't matter what everyone is doing. Is who you are, is what you value with your whole heart, and it should come to reality. Regardless of how everything is meant to be, let's not lose that tradition that we have of the world that we've seen. How you have known things are to be done, which excited you, and you became so full of joy and felt the need to call it a blessed life. We don't let that be taken away from the next generation, is what they should come to experience.

We pass that from one generation to another, and when you look at the new world that hasn't come to be content of the life that we living. We only wish to tell those stories that are important to their lives, of what are the true values of all that is love, and how they can make the most of it. We wish for so much to happen and now it has reached at that level, where if you want to see it manifest then give your true love to it. Do not wish for a certain world to be created if you're not ready to take part in the creation of it.

All that you require to see created, will come to be, only that you need to play a major role in the creation of it, if you want to see peace globally, then be there to make it happen as well. We need to have good households, partners, as well as children, then do it for them, and for everyone that you love, every child and human that we see on the street. Is exactly the reflection of what could come to be in our lives, so feel it as the most necessary thing that must be done to make the world a good place to live in.

Chapter Fourteen

What if I Knew

When the road gets rough you can blame yourself for doing something that you're passionate about. As situations do become a little difficult, and so much does turn into what you didn't expect. It is always possible that so many don't see the world in the same way as you, and they might think that striving to reach your innermost desire has anything to do with being comfortable. While a lot can insist on telling you how uncomfortable life is, and that if you want to move on in the direction of success, you must adjust to the way things are.

We at times fall in love with the world and our ambitions so much, it becomes the only thing we know how to do right, and when you devote yourself to doing it. Is not that situations are comfortable or maybe it feels good, things could be hard to cope with. It may be that with some goals that we want to see manifested it is necessary to live in our own creativity.

Even though you could still be weak in so many areas that it doesn't earn you the life you require now. You feel the need to hang in there, and to what you have chosen to be, and it could be important to hold on to what you have begun since it is your ideas.

Once in a while you could feel lost to all that is happening around you. It might happen that you're not the same to other people, and looking at yourself globally you do find your place through the love you have for your desire. You know what you're doing, though it might be taking longer than expected coming to light. You have accepted that as your only gift and you have to focus on it given that without being part of that, there wouldn't be any reason to live for.

We're all given different identities and we know who we are, though it might not have happened the easiest way to find your passion, and the need to be always involved in it. So much can say a lot about you on your way to success, but you acknowledge that it only became real through discipline. You did take your time off, and focus for something to become the reality you now live as your life.

We don't live to impress or be accepted by anyone, at some point even if it means that you go through the sacrifice to resemble your uniqueness, and regardless of the situations we could be facing at hand. Is our passion that matters the most, and when you're not fortunate to have started well. It must be something that you know you didn't do it for the world to appreciate you, is what you did to free yourself.

We have this prison that can live with us for the rest of our lives, and when you don't know how to free your life from that part. You remain there wondering about what you could have been, and that has resulted in you being lost, and now you lingering there longer than you've anticipated. You keep looking for the person that you were, and you cannot remember what you use to be, or see what to become.

You find yourself standing there not knowing when will you ever break free, and it so happens that whatever people can offer you will never be enough to help escape your situation. To come out of it means that you traveled through your understanding, and just like that you will make it to the other side where you can have everything that you deserve.

We find ourselves imprisoned from a lot that is life, as we live with the desire to be so much that we love or part of the world, and there can never be an easy way to be that. We become subjected to living our lives normally even when you've reached at a point where you're ready to break free, you feel pushed back to that place where you began. Regardless of how much you've given for something to happen, that which we seek the most always comes back to be what matters first to achieve before everything.

For a longer period so much can set you up with the same situation repeatedly that you can feel no need to be human, and is likely that when you engage in whatever you find necessary. You could've thought that you will easily manifest your ambitions, and you can't, you are forever stuck in that place where you've identified your goals. More like your life has now become a subject to something which is so difficult to understand or let alone achieve.

Like you haven't lived, you could have tried to be part of life and you never got a chance. As you couldn't reach for what you loved about yourself, though some situation might allow you a space to live at some point. Of which may not be enough to pass you through to the other side, and you manage to continue with it, still, a side of you remains a subject to that and you can't move on completely.

You become dependent on a situation that is hard to realize its success, and it has been the way you lived, you got caught up there trying to breakthrough your knowledge. Now you want to live a full life and the question that lies deep within you is, how do you pass such a situation and reach for your dreams, knowing that you can never be cursed beyond what you feel right now? There will be things that are meant for you to understand to be a free person, so when you have failed you keep on living at the same place you hate about yourself.

The fact that we sometimes have our fate decided for us before we are born in the world makes it all worse. Since on that part you don't have a choice to choose who you are and what to become. You just wake up in the morning and your life has been determined for you, and you have been pushed into a place that is not exactly where you are free.

What if you are birthed in a situation which the world is not yet content of with regard to the future, or where it is headed, and your mind could be independent from everything there is? Or maybe you might never have real opportunity to be all that is life now or to matter to whatever is going on. You are almost part of creation, not entirely, that condition which you came from become sort of a prison you have against so much that is happening.

Our minds exists where we're free from all that there is, and we are these kind of people living with expectations that we will reach where we see ourselves. Though you find yourself traveling in a situation that is not a very fortunate one, and to be found there is to be struggling with all of life, and is not like you stand against anything outside your world.

You just live with a vision to have what you intended from the beginning, and it has been a goal so hard to achieve. As we never give our lives to what we love completely, and you wander how you ended up living for your own creativity.

We are born with unique potentials, though is not something that exists on the surface, and to reach for it, you must give more of who you are. Learning to distinguish yourself from the other, and finding that uniqueness that you possess, and depending on how you feel about it. The love in our hearts can disappears at some point, to make way for that goal to be the foundation of all that we desire most.

As we are called into a world where we were destined to enjoy all that we are, and you can be happy with yourself, to be living in a world with endless opportunities. Although if you have an objective to live for, you won't have anything to rejoice about every day, given that for some time you might have nothing to show for. What you intended becomes your only way to have, and from that you can witness a brighter future.

With that passion so much meant that you have a significant role to play in the world, and for some time you might fail to find that. You can try to live in denial, somehow being part of that life will come to mean everything, and needs you to know more about what to do and how to be good at it. Is sad how so much about the person that you were can become meaningless.

As you are here to make a difference, and if you give yourself that opportunity to adapt to what you are. You will be the best in doing what you have been called for, even if the process to understand that won't be an easy one to the end.

It is a restless world and you will not know everything it requires from you, and how to get it done so easy, and what you actually did to start traveling on that path. Which has now become more like you have been cursed by the same dream which was supposed to make your life a better one, and yes it will happen the way is meant to be. Still, the fact that you have to create it until it becomes meaningful, living every day and going through time, doesn't become something comfortable to cope with.

The difficulties you can go through being the only thing standing between you and your best creation. Something that challenges the person that you are, achieving your deepest thoughts. The one thing that defines you, living by the only rule that makes up for everything that you wanted. To manifest your passion would mean that for the first time you will be free from the heavy load that has been dragging you down.

Though is not so much now, and instead of agonizing about it, you set your mind for the outcome to be success and do it. As it is what waste our time, to hesitate about what we truly need, you decide now if it makes up for what you really desire, and make it happen as the only thing that matters.

If you not living your passion, you will not be happy, regardless of what you know or want out of life, let it be what you desire most that you after. As scary as every day can be, when you wake up be focused on doing it more than you did yesterday and keep growing with it. Knowing that the world is vicious and will want to take everything from you, and we go through that to find happiness.

You can call it whatever you like, in your quest to understanding you walk through that passage to have your dreams realized. If it never spoke to your heart keep living the only life you have ever known, for those who know are meant for the world. They have accepted to be more, whether you try to hold them back or not they will find that space that allows for them to grow into what they desire most.

There are so many who knows how to live easy, to be themselves where they have seen life. You see what you like and do it, and you're grateful that you only need to hold on to being the person that you are. You are the kind of an individual who make use of the simple opportunities that we all have.

Who sees something that doesn't serve them and run away from it, that being how you preserve your values and you are prepared to live by that rule. Not so many have the courage to be what they like or to find themselves where they're stars, they fear the greatest sacrifice into understanding what they are on the subtle regions.

You begin to realize that you've found your love for the world and everything in life, and from that point where you discovered your purpose, a lot begins to mean so much. You learn to look away from what doesn't serve you, and that is how a definite goal changes you into the person that you happy about.

Knowing that you could have been living without consideration for what is happening around, or being aware of what is going on. As from now you are able to proceed through the vision you have define for yourself, you have identified the truth that you want to see, and is able to show you wrong from right.

You have discovered one of those gifts which becomes like a melody of your life that you live to sing. Living by such an objective, you not crying, you are yearning more from the world you have identified your goals. You keep talking about it, to yourself and everyone who cares, is that thing which its success, defines who you are and what you permanently stand for.

You could have had so many opportunities to live by, and you were never given a chance, don't be afraid that it came through the most unlikely thing, which to understand became everything.

For those who know the truth and believe in something special, the world needs your input, do not hesitate thinking that so much will get better along the way without you. Do not even waste time on things that are undeserving of your attention. This path is meant for you to look away from everything and come closer to the center where you're destined for more.

All that you got from the life you've been living is nothing, compared to what your understanding carefully analyzed can offer you. Do you think anything will ever change for greater tomorrow, or dream about any good happening without inventing it yourself?

If you don't believe in it, you can keep living the lie for everybody to accept you, and for what is worth it will not get you as far as you require. In the only life that you will matter, is through the gift that you have been given. You will be surprised by how much time you've lost doing something which even at the end didn't earn you so much, except that it ended up breaking your heart, find quality in everything that we live and love.

You could have thought that life will be a joyride and happiness will be easy to achieve. Unfortunately it didn't happen like that, for some time things could have went well, only that situations did caught up with you. In reality nothing is free unless you master the situation with your understanding, and avoiding the path can never make anyone love you. If they didn't care about you then, they won't start now.

So immediately you have seen yourself not happy somewhere or being liked the way you wanted to be appreciated, know that you are meant for the world or to find your talent. Deep within we are destined to find something worthy of our efforts, and regardless of situations being difficult as you have to learn so much.

Accept it as your path towards becoming a better person, the most upsetting thing is that we work hard to be understood and you constantly raise your eyebrows thinking that maybe this time. While is still the same outcome, if you had seen so much and life like that, would you deny yourself the truth living by your rules, that you have come to understand that your ideas are the only thing that matters?

Maybe you couldn't look away, as bad as situations can be when you have known and seen what the world became. Something did change within you to become what you didn't expect which is the person we see today on the outside, and once your life has been created by a reality you have witnessed. Is like a nightmare becoming real if you don't act upon it, and you cannot let things get out of hands.

Then we choose ourselves when things have been that bad, the thing is, that demon which is all over your life. Has spreader throughout your entire being and there is nothing of the world that we know which is remaining, and imagine if creation the way you had known things has been ruined. Man is having a run on all that which had been your rightful belonging, what would you do about it? We create our own understanding, and hope that it will be a better solution.

The same is everywhere, the gift that you are is the only reality that matters all over your life, and which can set you free from these things which are too costing for your happiness. Change does occur, if you live with the belief that you are searching for yourself, you will find the answer, though not in one day.

It will come back to make sense, don't think that you were never meant for what you will understand, as you are, and it will be the person that you become. Though you can feel like you're wasting a lot of time dedicating so much efforts to something which you know very well is important to you.

You could have been living so beautifully that you had been the best out of this life. Then something comes and ruins that from you, and now you can no longer remember who you had been, and you live with the regret. Beauty being held back against showing what you are. So much can steal away the tender that you just can't look away forever, and the most important part about it is that if your first love has been taken away from you, is not the end.

If you keep holding on to what you've lost, that doesn't create you, and moving on with life it might crush you down to nothing. While the real truth is that you should get out there, be a very strong and unique individual, confront situations and become something new. Change your cause and be a different person, from all that you've lost which you hoped would have been living happily. Invent yourself again, and you will see that nothing was taken from you, true love created by our own understanding never leaves you.

You only become better at what you are, so do well, be early to see this kind of things and seize your greatest opportunities. As it does exist that you might think your sorrow will be coming to pass, while it remains there, don't be late on the next chapter which is your new life permanently.

Is what you're meant for, and not to be sad when you can't have the present, it wasn't for you. Regardless of how hard you try, let go and stop holding on with everything that you have, as if you earning something out of it. You not gaining anything from that commitment, you are just suffering the embarrassment from lacking insight creativity.

Find true love for what you do, something that can hold you up, which is here to redeem your pride. After all has passed, that is what matters the most which you must remain with. We want so much, even though at times it could be hard to reach for it, in the world facing life without genuine knowledge, or creative intelligence. You can never be sure of what it is that you doing until you find your passion where you're knowledgeable. You can see so much being lived, as for you are only meant for what you know.

You can ask so many question, "what am I suffering from, why do I neglect myself so much?" You don't despise yourself. It could be that you haven't dedicated your life to something that deserves your attention. Given that it does happen that we can waste a lot of time on things that isn't who we are, or what can bring out the best in us, and you end up crippling your soul as you not growing forward.

At some point you may find yourself heartbroken that you can hardly remember how to be happy, and you wander how you ended up in that situation. Something has destroyed everything that you value and in a lot of areas your life cannot be fixed, and whatever you do is not recognized. Is when you know your efforts are unworthy, there is where you're meant to be, and you can be a human being and a different person, if you can only realize that a change is needed to become what matters to you.

What would you do when your heart has seen something and falls in love with it so much that it has become the only thing that you sing from deep within your soul? You can give the best that you have, look away from as much as there is in the present, if happiness is in the future, spend that much time trying to make everything worth living for.

What becomes the issue that you ought to have avoided is constant disappointments, you must be weary of trying to force things to happen. If it wasn't meant to disappoint you, then you would have been content of yourself by now. So find something which will not let you down, and focus on it as you have to live what matters at some point.

You can break your heart so many times going after the same thing as you want someone to make you happy, you want to be inspired to be something more. So if they don't bring that out of you, what would you do about it, how would you say "things will be better", as you do not know how to do anything for yourself?

Then you need to look deep within, and decide once and for all, if you will let human beings to forever be the ones that determine everything that you are. As it is what destruct so many before they can find their true self, they're holding on to others. You want them to be the ones that bring out the best in you, and you become sad when they cannot be there for you every day.

It could've happened in so many occasions when you failed, that you had been relying on outside influences as you haven't found your true passion for life and love. Something that enables you to stand straight, you have been holding on to family to give you strength, you don't have it inside, you break to pieces.

On the other side you depended on partners which are not giving you the best that you deserve, to just try a little harder on your own is to be free from all that exists. As it does happen that if you master a certain thing or way then everything you need will come through that path and is worthy.

You can make a living through your understanding, and when it has happened that you are not as good as you want to be, and certain things have destructed you. Which you don't know how they came about or how to pass them, how would you handle that part of life?

As it does happen that you have always known how to do things, not precisely that you are perfect at it, and you have so much going bad for you and you're meant to be on your own. How would you take care of that when there's no one around you, except that you have yourself to count on?

Although everything is better, you can make a habit of a life that you desire, yes is true you cannot say that you living when you're not in your ultimate form and capabilities. You keep practicing and doing it, everyone once in a while does get a chance to be recognized, not only for being the best. It could be for what you do or what you stand for, knowing that everything you do lacks that touch of perfection, and no one is there to give you advice.

You keep disappearing regardless of how hard you try, you end up being disappointed, is how low you can go when your abilities are not enough. If you never lose faith in yourself, you can have a chance to make a living through something which isn't what you had hoped for, as we are not all meant to be excellent.

The need to break out, you can pass through any situation without knowing how you came to be successful. Start right where you are to have faith in yourself, need family and that special person when is important. Though they cannot influence that much in what you can do, somehow they can help you realize where you are, love is holding on to being human. Is where you still matter to something, someone is there to see to it that you not completely mad over everything, and you're appreciated for what you are.

The ultimate goal, to be a human so full of life, is when you give everything that you are, to what you want to see. Regardless of whether you're best or better, that even when you think you not making it happen. Deep within your heart beat towards what you need most, and that is enough to get you from one place to another. As much as we all have our place, you have found yours, and form a good part of creation, and you're appreciated for that.

Be it that you find it hard to be a star, through what you are, you have managed to pass all levels of dependency with the abilities you have. Which could have been hard to arrive at, and you did it, you have reached at that stage of life where nothing is against you, or is there to hold you back.

It keeps giving you more, so when you want to be something, be free to do it without care of how capable you are. Reach for your own desire, walk out of that dependency and be content, it exists within every person whether you have so much or little potential.

You can have so much and still depend a lot on other people, but when you have done it right is your mind that breaks free. You no longer hold on to anything, you have arrived where you need to be and you are so full of life. Once you pass to the other side a lot will keep freeing you from all that has been holding you back. Is hard to push yourself and get there, only that life won't make any sense until you've done that.

It's a place of success created by your understanding, is beautiful and completely safe it doesn't hold on to anything, unlike in our ordinary lives where you wouldn't be what you choose to be. Is a part of you where you are free to be what you desire most and you are happy knowing that you are made by your capabilities.

Chapter Fifteen

A Shower of Diamonds

The reward seems so hard to reach for, like it doesn't ever want to come, it insists on being the most difficult to achieve. Can you be strong enough for it to happen, knowing that it will mean everything, while in the meantime or for a very long time you remaining in darkness? We work every day waiting for that initial moment where part of all that we've truly dedicated our efforts to, become physical. As you could've been this person who felt the pain of doing so much that is necessary to arrive at a point where your life must produce success.

Is never what you think you can achieve easily, and becomes so difficult to witness success. Somehow we feel denied of all that we worth, being someone who will once again be known for what they are or love about this life. It could have been easy if it was something that is within your control, now with this thing that we so eager to accomplish, you live with the burden of knowing that though you can do everything for yourself. You want someone's approval, who stands there and tell you that what you have done is enough.

As a beginner you feel the need for an expert advice, someone who approves of what you have done, and is there to honor your efforts. As it feels like we can crown our own work, or give ourselves thumbs up. Yet we lack that genuine knowledge that turns our hard labor into victory, is your first time, you haven't passed through it all.

You must be evaluated by others who are credited with this kind of understanding, you cannot be rejected by everyone. Regardless of whether you feel so small in a big world, you must allow yourself to grow, and reach at that level where your endeavors says so much about you, and that will earn you your star.

You must be worthy of being loved by human beings out there, shine among so many, and stand out from the crowd. As that's what we are, people striving for them to be the best, and for one to understand that you are better you must be comparing your talent with others. It could have been difficult to come up with a concept that will make you look different from the rest. Maybe taken so long to perfect it to that level where it will make sense to everyone, and we push ourselves to get to that point where everything becomes excellent.

Knowing that it wasn't easy, but something in you kept on believing. Even if it meant that it changes everything about you, and you must be that nature of an individual, who made it out of those kind of situations that are the most difficult to understand. Not that it was suffocating, it could be that it took everything from within, even discipline. You became focused, knowledgeable, and matured, you stopped hating what you are, and fall in love with yourself and your ambitions.

Now at the end when you know that you can no longer go back, you've invested everything that you have on this individual that you are. Maybe is not complete, we still need to give more than we have resembled, and to show a lot of courage than before. We don't give up now, we carry it inside, we put the love where is supposed to be, even though is so heart breaking that it became the only thing you know how to do. Remember that you mustn't be changed by situation as it will always be evident, that we feel the pain, and everybody has a point where they can become weary.

So don't be weary, or blame yourself for taking this path and think of quitting along the way, always remember once in a while, that it will say so much about what you understand. You want that one moment in history to define you, and what you stand for, we are represented by our hard works.

So it could be necessary that we might need to give all that we capable of, live with pride to be the kind of person you have chosen, don't go in there, not knowing what you in it for. Be convinced that it is everything you wanted, though we sometimes die inside, however that talent will bring life to you.

Remain with the will to go on, what it means is what you will understand when on a journey that no one can talk you out of. Knowing what you want and how the outcome will be, and being proud of yourself that you became what you didn't hope will happen easily? Although you couldn't be completely alone, part of what you do is not your responsibility, still, you can take care of what you truly know is yours to handle. You looked at yourself and saw where you fit in and what you deserve, so who can tell you what to do, or what is best in that kind of situation?

You loved yourself so much and felt very deserving, and that's how it is, we fall in love with who we are. You see something good in you and say this is the kind of thing that I need to live for. I want to embrace this human being that I am, with all that I know and understand about life. You discipline that, and focus your attention on being the best there has ever been, you not undermining the world outside. You just wouldn't be anything if you abandoned this, and you do acknowledge that the whole of humanity exists with talent.

Is just that you have to make a room for your own well-being, it wouldn't be a life if you didn't live it, and it wouldn't be love if you didn't give it to yourself first. You saw something admirable in you, and understand that this I will offer to myself, you too deserve to be part of everything that is worthy of living.

Continue to treasure your existence, show it to the whole of humanity, that though you would have loved to hold a lot about the world dearly. There was a part you wouldn't be fond of, as you had this to embrace, showing that kind of affection to you, knowing that it is the only star you have.

If it was not about that you could've got lost in so many ways, as failing to find ourselves is to miss the greatest opportunity of all that exists out there. So it start with you, it begins from underneath, and you come back with it, you not ignoring the world that lives, or what has been life. It has come to your attention at the earliest point to be concern about your understanding as well, and better if you realize that too early. As you don't know what you love, until you've fallen with yourself first.

You will be surprised what the world will reveal to you that if you really want to achieve true happiness, then find yourself. Everything is here for you and it is genuine beauty, you are the center of attraction, you mustn't be afraid to live it, after all we do get our rewards at the end for embracing that kind of understanding.

The universe is a big open space that wants people to occupy it, and every place is like that, it wants to be filled with human love. Every form of creation wants to be lived, and imagine what you almost looked away from, an opportunity to be living the best life as you wanted to be ignorant.

You mustn't ignore a chance to live a life that you find necessary to become a prosperous person. You could've lived with the believe that so much will automatically change and be better. Acknowledge that there's what you can do about it right now, and is to have faith in something reliable. Which is working hard for all that you know, and love about the world, and you will find it very difficult to except that at whatever point, you are your only remedy, for the hurting soul, in the path you became lost, you are the herdsman.

Believe in the only chance you have been given that you possess distinguished beauty, and you can never be happy if you don't share that with the whole of humanity, who live with the eager to see a new world. Be the one that saw through that window of opportunity and do great things with your life.

If you start now your turn will come to make everything happen, and you have to eagerly await that break, for all that you deserve to manifest, and is not about who you are. You need to have faith a little bit, that is about what you can do, as so many can see beyond your appearance.

Someone can understand exactly what you mean, you have to believe in a perfect world that exists. It wouldn't be impossible for the reason that you are alone, if is possible and is a way in life, then you can do it, and make everything physical like it was meant to be. Pass through every situation that there is, the sooner you realize that you are a very unique individual. You begin to create value in yourself, and that which you keep closer to your heart, can steal the tender we have to find its path to existence.

We have something that from deep within needs protection, which is more valuable than anything we have, and it could be very precious depending on what you know. Is what you have worked hard for, or thoroughly understand, and a lot will always be after that, it might require for you to keep a close eye.

Is who you are, what you have accomplished over the years and you may not see the reason why, and it is important, not only once. For the rest of our lives that we live to cherish everything that we've become. The knowledge we have, feels like the way will never be possible through it, or maybe it doesn't exist, and it does, it makes up for the greatest solution we have.

It comes in a form of a big celebration in the lives we living, more like Christmas or a new year, is that shower of your whole year's efforts. Only that is much better, as is to celebrate all your life's work, everything you've done comes down to one day, and in that moment is when it will be truly meaningful. Is hardly a world where you can find anything to be joyful about, if you haven't seen that part of you coming back to make you happy and crown your hard labor, so much will just be there to make you sad.

You awaiting for that hour of glory which is the only time when everything is beautiful, and you are able to confess how you got lost along the way. Maybe travel a route that wasn't even meant for you to have experienced, and now you've officially discovered your potential.

You never know what you are until you find your true desire, something that arouses your inner strength and comes to life through passion. Unlike being where you not completely sure of what you doing, which is to be confused and caged in your soul, and that gift you've invested yourself in becomes your only path to freedom.

You will understand a lot as you go along, and be sure that you take everything into consideration. As from what you've learned you will be able to do so much with ease, and gain recognition from that. Unfortunately there are those things which are just not made for you at all, and it doesn't have to be about who you are, it can be anyone, and it doesn't change how creative you are.

As you were able to create something magnificent, and your mind began to serve that particular thing, and you came back from where you could've got lost. The rest of the world outside your focus became unimportant, as you learn to let go of what you use to be, and you've managed to discover in you a talent which has become precious to value.

Though you had to trust that into someone's hands, as they're capable of doing what you cannot do for yourself, and they are confident you will take care of your life very well, and wait with patience until they return with a good outcome.

Like your being told that beyond this point you cannot cross and see what we do with your work, and we wait eagerly until we become weary, and feel so miserable, and that's the toughest moment in our lives. Where we have to resemble faith, in what has passed to the other side, and that period reveals our true self, is like they have allowed you to show your inner being.

Left alone feeling useless and abandoned with no hope of when is it going to be all good, or when will it be over. Losing touch with reality your real identity comes out, and that person is what you were and who you will be for the rest of your life.

We never know why we have to be patient or the need to hang in there. What you understand is that deep within the individual that you are it could be important, and a reflection of your faith towards everything that you stand for, and we carry it through.

Knowing that we striving to resemble our true self, all this time that you took to discover who you are and what you doing. Is part of what you will come to love as it will enlighten your life, and is what we mustn't hide from the world, as is our innermost being?

Is what will come to life, as weary as you may be, you will not understand what pushed you to light. Is the world that doesn't choose, it gives us what we need regardless of who we are. Only that there's a gap that exists between our destiny and the present, knowing that you have fulfilled your purpose all the way to the end.

Just within that period you're tested on every virtue that exist, and what came out of that is truly amazing. As your true self is revealed, the person that you are, cannot hide away any more, like your being interrogated, to find out what you truly are.

We feel tortured by situations and circumstances that we go through, and though we say that is difficult. You cannot deny the truth that what you are was revealed, and is what you know about yourself. Whether you hide away from the whole of humanity, deep within is who you are, you can try to create a room for change.

Still we are sent back to that place where we refuse to accept so much about ourselves, and is true you came out. What you know about your life from deep within, and blame the world for doing that to you.

So at the end is not like you were forced to do something you wouldn't be doing, you were pushed to accept yourself. The real you who live inside, and you don't even know how to be anything without that side of you. Though is not something that exists on the surface, whenever you're pressurized, is where you go back to.

So at times if you know how you came about, you understand as you couldn't fool anyone, is that part of you that made everything possible. Something that saw the way, and it can happen with everyone, at any point in your life. You can be faced with the decision to surrender to your inner being, and we ask ourselves countless questions, who am I? You are that one who saw the way.

You cannot fool the world, you can only blind yourself for denying the real truth about your life. Going out there the universe is filled with this huge force that questions everything that we are, and you could have arrived at that point of success knowing that is through hard work.

Somewhere inside you're not proud of all that you've done, some things you did along the way had been irrelevant to what you wanted to become. While there's what had been the cornerstone to what you became at the end, and whether good or bad, you want to forget about that, or crown with it.

It only occurred during a period where you had reached the end of all that you doing, yet humanity will not let you rest. You will have your crown the way it is, or accept yourself, you might not do it before the eyes of the world, still, there won't be any path that exist except for that one way that you've traveled.

So if you came through an honest route, you will not only be rewarded for what you've done. The results will be that no one can take that away from you, is what you worked for, that you get at the end, and is all that matters.

You might have thought that maybe we can deceive human beings, and you can't, they're the greatest force stronger than anything you've ever felt. They made you realize what you are, is you that you find at the end, no one else. It could have been hard to accept that about your life, and we could have like to say other things, like we were pushed by people to those situations.

They changed us into something that we not, always remember that what we are is right here, you are not the person that you thought you will be, you are this human being that you've always been.

You tried to hide in the dark, still, as broad as the universe is. Going out there is filled with different characters living the truth and all responding to this thing that you are. From that you don't have an option except to like that inner person whom you could've tried to conceal from human beings.

For a very long time you couldn't cope with situations as you feel so pushed to be something that you not. The world, people, life, can never turn you into what you don't know, you will only find it hard to accept yourself.

So don't convince anyone, except for yourself that you know your inner being that you will not fear to accept what you've always been even when you're pushed to the end of your life. So imagine if you have worked for greater good, that goodness is what you will find.

Everything that we are is multiplied, the rights that we have done being brought back to us multiple times. How great it is, to see all your kindness being repaid to you, if you can open your heart to what you've become over time you will understand. That there was no harm, is just that maybe you tried to change what couldn't be altered in you.

Is sad because that side which is you, at a deeper level of participation couldn't allow you to do that, is like we are so many on the inside. Each and every individual has their role to play, even though we not fighting, we just want to account for all that we do. If I am inspired to write about love, from what I've experienced through the years then I cannot just bail out on that. Is true love which has won inside, and it should get its own place and allowed to be the solution to all my troubles.

At the end we choose our lives, we might not have had that opportunity from that very moment when we began our journey. For some reason we have enough time to make our decision, and you have to exercise it wisely, as we are always pushed back to that situation, where we know is what we did. Regardless of what could be the issue, we do have our role to play, and our world to choose, or the type of life we want to live. So how far does our choices make a difference? As you have yourself to rely on, you could have not decided on how it began.

Now you can decide the ending, right there in that very moment, you can arrive at a decision that can guarantee your safety and no individual can master your understanding. You can come out forth, desperate moments will always push us to make difficult choices, still, what you are, and among so many is what you will get out of life. So can you choose your values carefully and make it out clean, as you wish it should be done.

The world at large, are you prepared for what it is that it will seek out of you? Knowing that you cannot give yourself beyond what you capable of doing, we offer ourselves, so if it seek for you to make it happen beyond your own will.

Can you make it happen, or work out the magic? The star that you are, not created by the whole universe. Made by your inner will, to go beyond the conscious level, and you can't give anything more than that. You have reached the end, so what do you accept about yourself, do you surrender to what you have always been, or you believe you can change?

As bad as situations can try to hold you back, can you find a new beginning, through your act of participation reach at that place where the world in you is innocent.

Where you are pure hearten, and everything about you is as good as brand new. For as much as things have happened you felt so dead, denied an opportunity to be a human being easily, and nothing made it any easier. It appeared as if someone was hoping to benefit from all this setback that you went through. While what you wanted was a stage to shine, throughout the whole world, and for the first time people will learn to accept something different.

As big as the world can be, you will have your initial day where you get to be what you love, and for the first time human beings will experience a different perspective, and when that happens. What becomes the magic of life, what in the wonder of the universe is being created, which is the new formation? What begins to live, and what dies, which is this thing that you became bored of, tired, and you had been waiting for this moment, which never seem to have come easily?

Regardless of what stands before you, all you need is that once in a lifetime opportunity to take center stage and stand out. You have waited for so long, and it never became possible, and don't forget that situations mustn't push you back to that place, where you know everyone think you deserve to be.

Even if is hard to change, however can you alter a little bit of what you are and be accepted, for what you really are, through your acts of participation. As we are meant to defy the odds, as difficult as it could be to beat them, you know with a leap of faith in the right direction you can do it.

We can fix all the mistakes that we've made and now is time to do something great, can one good done in the world rectify all the wrongs we have committed? Funny how situations happens, will we ever have a chance even if is just one shot to be what I knew that I deserve?

So much is just meant for people to give up, the way things will insist on being weak for you, everything is after all that you value, where do we die? Inside or outside, where did we experience the pain, does it have that eternal hold on you, that you feel as you try to move on with life?

If you were given an opportunity to be what you want, what would you do which maybe will make you happy? Is just that so much will not let you go free, and is there to disappoint you more every day, and now you are just left with nothing to live for. What were we, before we decided to become this new people that we are, which we have chosen beyond the surface of our lives, now that you want something new, and a very fulfilling life which you will come to love about yourself?

We were not much, that's why it is questionable, we lived, not with a definite purpose meant for the rest of our lives. Once we were people who questioned who they are, not that it was inadequate, it was not enough for all that you desired. It was a life that made you linger there, sorrow was in your heart, other than being a star there were other reasons why you started this journey, and it could be about both, good and bad reasons. You became tired of the person you had been, it was not serving any great intention.

Something was just taking all that you are away from you, and you search for yourself, and you don't know where to find that inner being. The solution became something which part of it as well isn't happening very easy, so where do we go when that part of ourselves which we never liked even for a single day dies?

What become of that life that you had lived, when the star that we were dies, it blast into pieces and shower us with diamonds, we are crown by our old self. So what's the glory that crowns the new self? Is the former person that knows your worth, respect for all that you have done, and at the end of the day it crowned your worthiness.

Chapter Sixteen

Live Again

From all that has happened, you still matter, you continue to be the most important person not only to yourself, to others as well. That is how far being an individual can have you traveling, and you can say that the most crucial part of everything that you've learned. Was to free you from your past, that's beside the need to succeed through the work you've been dedicated to.

So much could have been following you, and I guess there's nothing you could do about it, and is not like you are born bad or cursed. It is part of those things that you never got right, and that can never set you free from anything. It led to a lot of things being wrong, and now you need to be coming to change more about yourself and what you did, as a great deal has now turned into a setback.

Until you discover that special talent, a lot of things could have had a hold on you. We are not likely to be born as free people who are focused both spiritually and physically, that everything about us is just right. So much that we are and what we want to enjoy about life could be compromised, beyond what you can understand. It forms part of what you didn't care about, and we don't get to realize that about ourselves, and the impact it has, too early.

You only begin to understand when traveling your own journey, and it could have restrain your full potential to participate. If at some point you shy away from human beings then something within you wasn't right, and you needed to fix that. So that you can get a lot of things correctly as there could be so many wrongs, if you see yourself not being happy or free all the time.

You must possess a quality of life that was able to walk right throughout of everything to the end without looking back, and maybe at times when you seek to understand how far you've traveled. You could ask yourself, what are you doing with all that you know? And if you are making something or enough out of it, then you could keep on living the way you do, and if you haven't done anything that you love.

Then you need a new beginning, right from that very moment, you must begin somewhere. Work it out to a point where what you are right now, connects to so much that you need to be in the future. Until it becomes an ambition so strong is exactly what you want to live for, the rest of your existence.

Is true the person that you now want to be, must be a complete human being, who not only begins a new life. Someone who becomes enough for all that there is out there, as what you were wasn't adequate to give you what you needed, and is not discriminating what you had been. You don't want to begin a certain path and fail to reach the end that is not really changing anything about yourself, even the past could still have a hold on you.

To be held back from the present, with so much that you wanted to be part of, only that for now you don't fit in. You are not worthy enough to be a person with everyone else, regardless of how hard you try, something just isn't right about what you are. You got left back and you working on becoming a new being.

You are meaningless to what is currently happening, and you search for yourself so deep and you don't find who you are, and you need to work more to discover your inner self. That unique thing which is the individual that you will appreciate, as what you were is not what you loved, and you cannot allow that to be what continues to see the world.

You need a quality of life so strong, that connects to everything that matters, and enlightens your world. It doesn't have to be a common path that humanity traveled to the stars, it could be your own. As we differ so much as human beings and to be happy you might need something that speaks directly to your inner being, and that becomes enough to lead you to the destiny you desire. What would you do if it wasn't a thing that you possessed, and you want to become an important person, as you cannot wait and watch forever?

You are not enough until you take a moment and dedicate all that you are right now and what you've known to a special purpose. What would it say about yourself for the rest of your life, would things had been good, knowing that you wanted more out of this world? As you have it in you and know that much, and you had been conscious of everything that exists around you, and you were never part of it.

However this is one of those things that you chose among everything, as the ultimate rule and passion for what you desire that you're prepared to live through. As you need something worthy that you can call living, and no matter what everybody does to stand against that, they cannot stop you in your new path.

There's what you find in you to be the only path that exists, and is part of those things which you can't compromise. There is just no other option and you know that you can't be something else, and you understand this isn't shopping the choices are very limited. What you discover in you could be the only thing that you are, you can work for what humanity is and see that gift you have disappear, or you can be creative and live through your understanding, and head for it.

You know when you reach for that thing which is just who you are, and if you were not that, you wouldn't be happy as it would be living a lie, and from doing what you love you cannot be left with so much to be elsewhere.

You do a certain thing with passion hoping that it turns into a masterpiece of creation. You take everything that you are and all that you love and put it right at the center of your focus, until it reaches at that point where it is good enough to confront the world with. Though you don't know what could stand in your way, for so much that you understand. You wish for the best to happen through that path, still, something can be tempted to disturb your progress so bad you can fail to make sense of what you had been.

We are never that guilty, but you cannot know everything about life and yourself, and if something refuses for you to be normal in society. Then so much could be wrong, and we are all enough, maybe different in some ways, and without understanding what could have gone bad. Situations can stand before you and judge as if you inadequate to make a living through the simplest path available to everyone, and that's why you need a new route, one where you show everything that you capable of.

Your path must lead to a better place, where everything that you are is accepted, and you are what the world is and though you might stand out a little bit. Only through understanding, and that says so much about an individual, to do things which are not quite usual to get where you are person. You are not exactly how everyone is, even so you don't need to be excluded from life the way it is, especially necessities that contribute to being normal in society.

We are all human beings that live for the same thing, and if you don't have that, you feel useless regardless of what you want to be or aiming at. So much can pass through you, and with you, and after some time your mind is not there anymore, and you might need to pull your attention back to focus.

Once you feel yourself fading from your desires, you could be required to put that much energy into what you know has always been the key to success. We don't look for ourselves out there, we are here, and within our reach, you just have to find something that matters to you.

When a need arises, you must be very prepared to do exactly what is expected of you, we sometimes have a period in our lives where we must prepare what we know. Regardless of what it is that you do it needs to take form, as we are only given a limited chance before we are required to show what we understand.

We are never free all the way, time comes and we must be able to account for so much that we are, and when that happens you ought to prove that you can rely on yourself. As that's what will say a lot about you, against everything that we encounter daily.

If you not certain that what you know can take form through your understanding, then you still have faith in something else. Refuse to be tied down to things which are not what you want, believe in yourself a little more, and enough to carry your desires to a level where they are formed.

It works all the time, as you gain confidence you begin to pass levels that measure normality, and you can never remember that you were once stuck. So if part of you still hope for answers to come from the world outside, then you are not ready to be a star, you're standing somewhere lost and not doing it the way is meant to be.

You become equipped with knowledge enough to be someone who is ultimately the best thing that has ever happened, and above all that you've known. Is like each time you have a choice to choose between two entities you see yourself as the greatest that there is, you cultivate that much faith in your capabilities. How would you justify the eager you have for everything that is life if at some point you were not the excellent option to what is available?

You work to create something strong and better to confront the world with. You just not going to waste time forever pretending that maybe you would've been different, and you would have made any impact, living in a reality that you not happy about.

The old self is not earning you anything in return, stop convincing yourself and other people out there and say "you sorry to be late, and not doing it alright, you will try harder." There is no need trying hard at what everybody is, after you've found something so unique, you delaying your progress. You have to do a real soul confrontation, is that moment where you are required to say it out, and it becomes easy.

Like that it is time, for it to happen at its natural state, unlike how you feel being edgy, to be a star is to be sure of what you are. You not in that point in your life where you standing knowing that you shaking from not understanding what you must do.

You possess knowledge enough to free you, you're at a level where you excelling and it doesn't require that much from you. Except that you have done all that is necessary to be there, you have reached that quality of understanding. By giving everything to what you doing, and you proud of it, and if you were ashamed, where else would you find yourself. As people who feel like that are still hiding somewhere underneath them, and you wouldn't be that weak if you want to manifest your true desires.

Over time you embody that eager to be outstanding, you let go of the fear you feel inside, you cannot fail in everything. There is where you need to be strong enough to take a stand, something in you must be human otherwise you wouldn't be fit to walk out here in the world with other people.

If you outside here and you walking normally then you still possess that quality we call life. Though it could be hard to reach and resemble that towards other human beings. Somehow if you can find a center where you focus your attention it can become the shape of your reality.

To reach your full potential you need to stop being a bystander, and take a stand, that's the thing, you always allowed people to be the ones that take center stage, as you think you don't know much. At times you must accept that we all have an obligation to do something to be normal, everyone is meant for that one moment in life, which is just for you to say it to be human. No matter how shy you are, once in a lifetime you have to tell that special person "I love you" to live happily ever after, and someone must join you and say "I love you too".

One has to give in to what you are, once in a while you have to stand there and speak for something that you believe in and seek to be clearly understood by everyone. No matter how caged you could be in your own understanding, it is evident of all human beings that is what we are in a lifetime. People striving for clarity and to be heard, we only delegate if it wasn't our responsibility, so whatever you doing must be preparing you for that moment in life, as it is the gateway to fullness.

Let's say that you can still be a human being not sure of what you doing, or maybe you are that person whose shy about standing up for what they are, is not like you don't have it within, you do. We all have something equal to each other, and is that thing of not understanding where exactly you need to be, that robs us of everything that we know and understand about ourselves.

More like something is taken from you to increase on what someone is, since they need to represent you as well. Though there comes that time when it is just your moment to be precise, and nothing must be subtracted from your life. You have to be excited about it, and show that you are able to stand for yourself, how can you make peace with being a human if you haven't done your part?

It is your time and there's nothing missing, it says so much about the kind of people that we are, to have the same responsibilities. If you think you not capable of sitting there and talk about yourself, then you lack confidence. If you can't stand there and explain something more to human beings, then you don't have a clue.

The thing is that you need to have an idea of what's going on, you must understand, and see the reason why you have to do it, to come alive. We all possess the same qualities, is just that we want to know where, when and why, that's at the end of the day, where you're pushed to represent your opinion.

Through your understanding you must have all the qualities of life coming to play in you that must be possible. You cannot remain hidden, and sad when you haven't accepted that about yourself. When you still think there are some things you wouldn't do as you don't know how to be a human enough, that's an excuse to remain in one place.

Like it is said that you there, then act like it, with all that it takes and required out of a human being, it's easy to comprehend, you are here to say your mind, to represent your agenda. The world doesn't require anything else, if you're afraid to stand freely it feels like it isn't your place, or it was never where you belong.

In your territory find your part, what you possess, and feel normal to do it, as it is now time to be that. Put everything behind and look into it, how would you keep justifying the life you supposed to be living if you not there enough for yourself to be content, and take pride in it.

When that pride exists in you, it doesn't matter what occasion it could be, you are not afraid of the world outside. You are meant for every occasion at hand and if you don't do it for the people, then be that for yourself, not allowing that life to pass through you, will be that you never lived.

So you understand that when you had been unable to stand your ground normally you became unproductive, and ineffective enough. Now you see what you have failed to be in the world, to live means so much, and yes a lot can refuse for that in you to come alive and be a character that you possess and thrive through.

However is what you are as well, you are that human being, you cannot hide away from life. You taking your rights to be normal and express yourself accordingly, and you never know how much you have given up until is time to reconnect with everything again.

To be discontent of so much that is happening around you and what you want can never give you peace. You have to understand something which is focused on being successful, and allows you to have your way with everything that you need and what you feel that you can be, and you could have refused to grow. Fortunately now through your creativity, there's a lot that can come to life, and is more than you have ever hoped for, don't doubt it as is what you deserve, if you think is not part of what you are.

Who's going to live it for you, or be what you refuse to be, is what we take away from this beautiful creation. Through the responsibilities we have, and it becomes our share of life, you get to play your role, to earn your worth. It is something that you are happy to be in the world as well, from all that is available or which you have ever done. This is what speaks volume, and you cannot deny yourself an opportunity to be so much, or more than you have ever dreamed of.

Get inside your head, and talk to that thing which drives you towards your ambitions or the person that you are, to look at the world that we have with positive attitude. As some-thing's you can change while some you can't, and learning what is right from what isn't meant for us to be part of, and stick to what will keep you focused on being the best.

You could have gone through everything along the way, and you haven't find any meaning from what you have been, and now you understand why the need to pay attention to your own creativity.

You don't know what you looking away from, though is your own understanding, it could be the only way to free yourself. Regardless of the need to mature or grow, at some point you must seize those opportunities and be sure that you living for what will satisfy your entire existence. We are our only hope out of any situation, you can't be lost in vain forever, and you need to find that inner calling for something that will expand your world beyond expectations.

So much can change those assumptions we have for everything that exists, but by being over prepared. We are well equipped for all that can happen, and you find yourself thriving through any adversary. Against how impossible things can turn out to be, you've brought the best of what you are, to help you understand a lot on this surface. Which requires one to have worked beyond to stand apart, and you are able to remain strong in that as well, and there's no need for someone to come and take your place.

You might not be that person who is confident enough to take a stand whenever an occasion arises. You feel safe from exposure having to refrain yourself, deep within you it doesn't feels like it is your place. Remember that regardless of how you see the world, you don't have to criticize those who know how to be always upfront and doing things when people are unable to.

One has to do it, life becomes possible through these acts that we have towards creation. That is what could have had you remaining behind in so much, as you didn't see the need to participate in whatever there is around you, and to a lot of people that is living. If you never became part of it, they think of you as if you don't matter, or productive enough, and whatever you do doesn't amount to anything. Things have been like that needing you to stand up for what you believe in to create a space for growth.

For when that day comes you must be able to carry your responsibilities, and you are never required to do that until your time has come. Nothing ever pressurizes you regardless of the fact that you could be holding yourself back. As you not leading your life into a better place and you needed to have done so much for you to fit into situations and society.

We are those kind of people who are required to have understood so much about their lives. There is being involved with everything whereas at times you can be absent from all that matters, and regardless of how much you try you cannot undo that part you neglected about yourself, and so much can turn against you.

Until it becomes imperative that you have to play your part, no one can be there for you forever. You only have yourself, to walk through every situation, time passes and what use to be reliable becomes unimportant to put your trust on. So much losses value as you go along, and you remain with what you've turn out to be over time.

You feel the need to be something that you're meant to be and there's no part that you can undo about how you see yourself achieving your goals. You let that be the driver, leading you towards the direction you long to travel to reach your destiny, and you look away from everything, and that is how is meant to be. Is life on the path to your deepest desires, and through that you become a human being, it can never be that you didn't play your role.

Those who are prepared to live go through that road, their whole lives are filled with responsibilities, and to avoid that is to be lifeless. Be content of so much that is happening around you, not at some point, all the time, you just have to give everything up to make it happen. The standing far from whatever is going on doesn't work forever, at some point so much must pass upon you by being involved in it.

Immediately you are an individual you must speak for all that you have, and I guess that's what the world has an audience for. Someone who has a part of themselves which human beings don't understand very well and they seek clarity, and that's for everything we've become, and people cannot look away from that as if it doesn't exist.

You cannot stand in the corner and pretend not to see what you are, unless you're thief, hiding away from everything which is part of the crimes you have committed. We can be given what we worth or get all these kinds of good treatments from everyone. Only that you need to have deserved such warmth, by letting that character come alive in you, and that's what people have a room for.

You never gave yourself a chance, and you were not given an opportunity, as time comes in our lives, whereby what we say doesn't matter anymore. Is what we have and how we have done it that speaks volume, and it makes sense for things to be like that. You cannot hide away forever, you need to wake up from that deep sleep and come back to reality. Just to be sure that you are what you reflect to everyone.

You must know the path you traveling where things are how you have predicted they would be, and you mustn't just speak for what you wanted to be. You must be speaking for all that you are, what you were, and the road you have traveled, and where you still need to get to. What gives you the strength and motivation that you find in doing so much that you love, and that is where you derive the power to stand and represent everything people have never hoped you'll be?

We have had a long run and so much that we are, or part of our lives we cannot show for, and that's what makes it sad, that there was a lot that we couldn't express about ourselves. You suffered the strain for that, and it can never end like that. It only comes to make sense when you're clearly understood, and your level headed with everyone, believe that it can be done as failure to do so will not allow you to have peace.

Something must be there that justifies the life we live on a daily basis, and everyone must understand and be convinced of how we do things, and that's how it will make sense at the end. It must be able to give you that satisfaction, and everyone must find themselves in that context of your achievements. Otherwise, you cannot say that you know what you doing, become successful and never be proud of how you achieved that.

So much can try to steal what you have, since you have dedicated a lot of efforts to it. Only that we are different from each other in so many ways, and we live in separate worlds, and by being more focused to what you do, you differentiating your universe of understanding from others who exist out there.

Like it said about us people, we're just the same creatures living on the same thing, and though we try hard to think differently from others who live like us. Still, so much can have a hold on you as you try to create your own way of thinking.

Going ahead we suffer the strain as we needed so much, and we cannot be those kinds of people that we want to be so easy. We wanted to reach for the stars, someone who lives in their world, and that's sad as you cannot say so much about yourself so far. Sometimes we just live with it as our own thing somewhere deep within us that you can feel like you can die for it since you cannot tell anyone how you feel when is not happening.

For what it's worth, when it reaches the end, and you have done things accordingly, it must produce a similar outcome. That complete sense of satisfaction out of life, for you and everyone.

End!!!

About the Author

Sibusiso Malvin Tshabangu Born 7 October 1986, South Africa. Studied at the Tshwane University Of Technology with a B Tech: Degree In Marketing. My books are solely based on my research which I have conducted for over twelve years, after completing my studies, which I later had a breakthrough in Pharmaceutical studies, which became my area of practice, however choose to focus mainly on life and relationships as a reflection of my understanding, which emphasizes on the fact that to avoid a lot of what we can define as diseases and medical disorders, man and woman should learn to focus on love, even if you can be a Master in life, on its own knowledge cannot do that much, love completes everything that we are.

The Series Stars Do Fall in Love

Part One: *Individualism*

Part Two: Fame

Part Three: The Lady at the Centre of my Heart

www.ingramcontent.com/pod-product-compliance
Ingram Content Group UK Ltd.
Pitfield, Milton Keynes, MK11 3LW, UK
UKHW020143250726
13967UKWH00002B/825